MASTERS OF INNOVATION

BUILDING THE PERPETUALLY INNOVATIVE COMPANY

UPDATED EDITION

LID Publishing Ltd
One Mercer Street, Covent Garden
London WC2H 9QJ

31 West 34th Street, Suite 7004,
New York, NY 10001, US

info@lidpublishing.com
www.lidpublishing.com

A member of:

BPR
Business Publishers Roundtable

www.businesspublishersroundtable.com

© A.T. Kearney 2015
© LID Publishing Ltd. 2015
1st edition published in 2015, 2nd edition published in 2015

Printed and bound by CPI Group (UK) Ltd, Croydon CR0 4YY

ISBN: 978-1-910649-40-4

Cover and page design: Laura Hawkins

MASTERS

OF

INNOVATION

BUILDING THE PERPETUALLY INNOVATIVE COMPANY

KAI ENGEL, VIOLETKA DIRLEA, JOCHEN GRAFF

LONDON   MONTERREY
MADRID   SHANGHAI
MEXICO CITY   BOGOTA
NEW YORK   BUENOS AIRES
BARCELONA   SAN FRANCISCO

TABLE OF CONTENTS

PREFACE

When we first launched the Best Innovator competition in Germany in 2003, our goal was to identify and communicate the best practices of some of the most innovative companies. We hoped to show that German companies were still able to compete with emerging low-cost competitors from across the globe, based on their superior innovation management capabilities.

Now, more than 10 years later, the Best Innovator competition has been rolled out to nearly 20 countries, including the United States, most European countries, Brazil, Russia, and China. We have identified the most innovative companies worldwide as well as their best practices in innovation management. And with 10 years of research behind us, we have established a strong correlation between superior innovation management capabilities and sustainable, profitable growth. Best Innovator winners are living proof of this. Moreover, our research shows that over the past decade, the topic of innovation has moved from a top 10 position on the CEO agenda into the top three.

This book was written with an objective in mind similar to the one we had in 2003: to identify and share leading practices in innovation management as applied by the Best Innovators. We go well beyond the reams of data accumulated after a decade of research to also provide firsthand insights from the C-level executives whose companies have topped our list of winners over the years. You will learn from senior executives at Ferrari, 3M, Whirlpool, Henkel, and Volkswagen (to name a few) that innovation is a repeatable process that can be studied and perfected by systematically applying five true and tested value levers.

We are confident that even in today's dynamic, ever-changing world, *Masters of Innovation: Building the Perpetually Innovative Company* brings fresh thinking to the pursuit of innovation—fresh thinking that we believe will be relevant for decades to come. We wrote this book for all senior-level executives and management teams, but especially for those who want to achieve real and tangible improvements in their innovation endeavors.

CHAPTER 1
MEET THE MASTERS OF INNOVATION

Innovation is not an art. It's a capability. The past 15 years have brought a flood of how-to books about innovation, most of them replete with stories about startling eureka moments and charismatic leaders. These stories are fun to tell but usually have little to teach other organizations about building their own innovation capabilities, other than to hope lightning strikes or to hire a colorful CEO. Missing from the stories are the mechanics of what it takes to make innovation more than a breakthrough moment that lets a company ride a fleeting lucrative wave.

Masters of Innovation: Building the Perpetually Innovative Company shows that being innovative is a repeatable process that can be studied, learned, and practiced—one that will sustain a company's profitable growth for decades. This book is a manual for creating a permanently innovative organization, deriving lessons for best practices from the experiences of senior teams at Best Innovators—members of a select team of companies that come in all sizes and from all industries around the world.

The Best Innovator competition was first held in Germany in 2003. A.T. Kearney partnered with the German business magazine *WirtschaftsWoche* to recognize companies that were not only best in class in their products and balance sheets—though they were that too—but had also achieved success by building an organizational machine for sustaining innovative behavior. This book describes the levers of the innovation machine and how to pull them.

We focus on several types of innovation, from product and process innovations to business-model and service innovations. But they all have one thing in common: they all start as ideas and become market reality. And none earns the title "innovation" until it is making money.

THE BEST INNOVATOR COMPETITION
The Best Innovator competition began in Germany in 2003, partly in response to rising concern among Western European incumbents that more sophisticated—and lower-cost —competitors from emerging nations were threatening their long-range profitability,

and perhaps their survival. Contest organizers wanted to spotlight great innovators to show how innovation is done.

Now held in nearly 20 countries including many Western European countries, the United States, Russia, Brazil, and China, the competition has yielded a wealth of insights into how to excel in innovation management. This annual benchmarking against the best in innovation management focuses on the how-to of innovation and takes a deep look at what leading companies are doing to achieve better yield with their innovation strategies.

Every entrant begins with an online questionnaire. In this self-assessment, applicants describe their innovation strategies and the level of active support for realizing it, starting with top management. They also have an opportunity to provide more information about innovative approaches within the company or business unit.

A panel of judges analyzes the questionnaires and assesses innovation using both qualitative and quantitative criteria. The assessment measures crucial factors such as whether a culture of innovation is embedded within the organization. It is centrally concerned with the rigor and impact of processes for managing the innovation life cycle. Above all, it inquires whether innovation is continuous and successful.

From these initial entrants, those with the highest scores are short-listed for site visits by A.T. Kearney partners, which often include eye-opening discussions with CEOs and their innovation-management teams. After the site visits, winners are chosen using a structured assessment system based on both the questionnaire and the site visit. Winners are chosen by a panel of prominent judges drawn from industry, academia, and government. (To ensure no conflict of interest, A.T. Kearney is not part of the panel.) Win or lose, a confidential analysis of the innovation mechanisms is delivered to each contestant at the end of the competition.

In a little more than 10 years, the competition has grown to include nearly 20 countries. In that time, about 2,000 organizations have entered the competition. *Masters of Innovation* shares the lessons we've learned from observing all of them, not just the winners.

This book doesn't offer frameworks or bulleted lists. It offers the real experiences of the world's Best Innovators. These are not just the hot companies of the moment. On the contrary, they are often growing in traditional businesses—automotive, rail transit, household appliances—where slow growth would be expected. Many have been in business for generations, and still they grow.

Compare that record to the churn among members of the Fortune 1,000, which saw 60 percent of its list change between 1993 and 2003, the year of the first Best Innovator competition.[1]

Shareholders in Best Innovator companies have enjoyed the benefit of this commitment to profitable long-term growth. Since the competition started, the Best Innovators' shares have outperformed not only their peers, but also the stock market (see figure 1).

Figure 1
Innovators rise above stock market averages

Share prices
EURO STOXX 50, January 2003 to September 2014

¹Unweighted average of all publicly traded Best Innovator winners in France and Germany between 2005 and 2012
Sources: Thomson Reuters Datastream; A.T. Kearney analysis

COMMON VIRTUES

Best Innovators are often companies under pressure. Sometimes they face a threat of commoditization to a core product, or they might be contending with new entrants or an upstart technology. Yet what is remarkable is that their innovation strategies are not reactive. Their strategies are forward-looking and constant, open to course correction but clear in their destinations, through good times and bad.

It is telling, for example, how often Best Innovators have created their own adaptation of 3M's New Product Vitality Index (NPVI), which measures the

> "Innovation is 5 percent analysis and 95 percent fast and focused implementation. Profitability is required to invest in growth areas because our company has relatively limited resources."
>
> Rolf Hollander
> Chairman
> CEWE Color Holding

percentage of revenue derived from products launched in the past five years. For Best Innovators, a key performance indicator (KPI) such as NPVI is not a backward-looking accounting tool. It is an in-flight gauge that measures the progress of an entire innovation portfolio, a fact-driven view into what's working and what needs course correction.

Best Innovators share common virtues. For all of them, integration of process and deep-rooted innovation cultures are character traits. Best Innovators are always in a state of future-mindedness, and they don't get blindsided by change.

Consider CEWE Stiftung & Co. KGaA (German Best Innovator, 2010). From its start in 1961, CEWE spent decades among the leading European film-processing companies and was a rival to worldwide brands such as Fuji and Kodak. But film photography—analog—is now a niche business. For the past 20 years, the incumbents have struggled not only to respond to the advent of digital picture-taking but also to survive.

As once-great names have left the photography business, CEWE has grown. Better than its rivals, CEWE perceived in the 1990s that digital photography was, to risk a cliché, a disruption that would upend a well-established business model. It invested heavily in digital photo-finishing capabilities while its core analog business was still growing—a strategic choice that brought some initial internal resistance. Even as digital photography was becoming the dominant consumer technology, CEWE prepared for the transformation the Internet would bring to the old model of developing photographs through the mail or at the local pharmacy. As early as 1994, it was taking steps to provide online photo finishing and a range of customizable consumer products such as calendars, posters, and even canvases. Most important to sustained growth was the 2006 introduction of the CEWE PHOTOBOOK, built on CEWE's historic base of retailers. Since then, the company has sold millions of photobooks.

One day, these successful innovations will reach the end of their life cycles. CEWE wants to be ready when they do. It keeps a close watch on trends that may affect its business and predicts that the next big opportunity will come from mobile devices.

Figure 2

R&D spending does not automatically boost profits

Correlation between R&D spending and EBIT in select industries
(as % of sales)

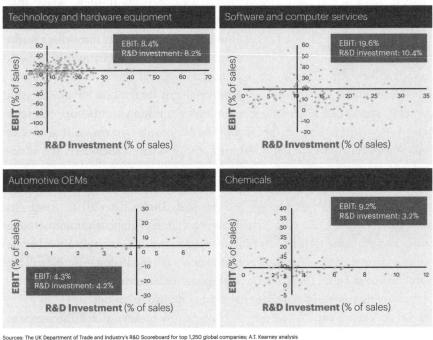

Sources: The UK Department of Trade and Industry's R&D Scoreboard for top 1,250 global companies; A.T. Kearney analysis

"Innovation is 5 percent analysis and 95 percent fast and focused implementation," says Rolf Hollander, CEWE's chairman. "Profitability is required to invest in growth areas because our company has relatively limited resources. We need to focus on major areas for growth and define the right innovation search fields."

IT'S NEVER ABOUT BRUTE FORCE

The list of Best Innovators includes several incumbents in large industries. Whirlpool, 3M, Ferrari, Coca-Cola, and Volkswagen are just a few of the big companies you will meet in *Masters of Innovation*. But from the beginning, what has distinguished the Best Innovator club is the diversity of businesses and the range of sizes. Among the most compelling stories are those of two mid-sized Czech companies: LINET, a $160 million maker of advanced hospital beds with just 800 employees, and ČKD, a 2,000-person firm that steadily reinvented itself in the 25 years after the Cold War from a struggling maker of tram cars into a forceful world presence in energy engineering and services.

The lessons learned from Best Innovators are not dependent on business interest, size, or region. For example, in the analysis on page 13, developed from publicly available data, it is striking that there is no correlation between R&D budget and innovation (see figure 2).

Again, there is no link between money invested in R&D and profitability, measured by earnings before interest and tax (EBIT). Profitability is the reward for doing the right things in the right way.

Hard figures from Best Innovators reveal that it's not how much you spend but how you spend it. For these organizations, innovation is not a factor of brute force—lots of budget, lots of time, lots of people—any more than it is the fruit of some eureka moment. Innovation for them is a management capability and a repeatable process.

To get their innovation strategies right, Best Innovators invest up front in understanding market, technology, and service dynamics. They are investing time more than money. Once they have innovation strategy right—not just on paper but in the minds of all their most influential internal decision makers—they begin collecting the ideas that have potential into a managed portfolio. We call this portfolio *search fields*. These are the wellhead of the innovation flow.

Sometimes, we characterize the Best Innovator philosophy as "from the market to the market." What this means is that innovations in embryo emerge from close attention to the market—the voice of the customer—often before the market knows it is saying anything at all, as was the case with digital photography for CEWE. The early work on an innovation portfolio is the collection of ideas that flow from this attentiveness. We describe this as the "desired-outcome approach" to idea development, one that frames the market's appetites in terms of what customers need. Managing these ideas depends on a rigorous connection between them and corporate strategy.

EMOTION AND FACT

We don't minimize the intellectual and organizational challenges of managing an innovation portfolio that is loaded with ideas. Throughout this book, when we talk about managing an innovation portfolio, we are not just talking about one idea nurtured from market insight to product launch. In reality, there are hundreds of embryonic product ideas in a large corporation, dozens in a smaller one, and all at different stages of their life cycles. These ideas overlap and influence one another. The overlap and influence are managed in terms made explicit in the organization's culture and processes.

Another way of talking about culture and processes is to talk about emotion and fact. Best Innovators have a visible organizational desire to balance these two elements in creating a foundation for recurrent innovation. Naturally, a clear and convincing vision is needed to excite a company's culture (and shareholders). But without a fact-based argument to realize the vision, excitement is not enough.

To balance emotion and fact, Best Innovators navigate a natural tension between flexibility and control. The tasks of control—progress tracking, coordination of innovation and functional strategies, deviation analyses, control of planning premises and processes—make excitement about the vision tangible. The devotion to KPIs and rigorous stage-gating so typical of Best Innovators allows them to give their organizations a distinctive degree of freedom, a kind of structured autonomy that encourages creativity and the birth of new businesses.

> *"In line with Schumpeter's theory of creative destruction, innovation can also include the decision to leave behind some areas of the present business. It is not only about doing new things but also about getting rid of traditional products, services, and even companies. Otherwise, we could not afford to invest in new areas."*
>
> Georg Kapsch
> CEO
> Kapsch TrafficCom

Every organization has its cultural norms, unspoken or not, for good or for ill. Members are attuned to what is valued, and they behave accordingly. If culture is the sum of what is prized, then the culture's norms should prize innovation. This is how Best Innovators create an environment where smart people thrive.

"You build a foundation for innovation," Hollander says. "Prerequisite is a culture with an open mind that stimulates employees to come up with new ideas by ensuring a certain level of freedom. You want them to dare to take risks."

Without structure, there is no creativity—a fact seen again and again in the way Best Innovators first develop and then manage their innovation portfolios. All of them pursue clarity on a fundamental question: what do we want our innovation strategy to do for us?

Consider Whirlpool Latin America (Brazil Best Innovator, 2010). The company is the leader in Latin America's home-appliance market and a growing part of Whirlpool Corporation's revenue. In 2008, Latin America contributed 19 percent of the parent company's total revenue. By 2013, that rose to 26 percent. Whirlpool now has the top market share in the region.[2]

By the standards of Best Innovators, Whirlpool Latin America's innovation management system is still young. It was developed in the mid-2000s in response to what the company saw as an emerging trend toward commoditization and price reduction in the appliance business. Convinced that customers would pay a premium for genuine innovation, Whirlpool was deliberate in building an innovation culture. Senior leaders were assigned an annual innovation pipeline target. But how would that be measured? How could anyone tell if what was in the pipeline had long-term value?

To earn the status of potential innovation at Whirlpool, an idea must make its case. First, it must contain a compelling proposition for customers and be aligned to the company's brands. Second, it must create durable competitive benefit—in other words, it must make use of Whirlpool's patents, technology, distribution, brand strengths, corporate scale, or some other advantage unique to Whirlpool so that competitors cannot follow for at least two years. Finally, a new idea must offer the prospect of serious shareholder value.

Senior leadership's first move was to define innovation in a context particular to Whirlpool. A common definition creates several benefits: it avoids time-wasting discussions about what is meant by innovation and clarifies the goals of the innovation strategy. It also generates KPIs to assess the performance of the innovation portfolio and the performance of those managing it.

The results are in the numbers. Today, the portfolio of Whirlpool Latin America's products classified as innovative is responsible for one-fourth of its revenue. These products are on average two to three times more profitable than the rest of the company's product line.

Best Innovators answer the questions that matter, beginning with the mechanisms by which innovation can deliver long-term profitable growth. They can name the market segments where they will concentrate their energies and the competencies they will need to acquire, buy, or borrow to succeed. They match this *inventory of competencies* against their talent-development strategies.

DRAWING THE ROADMAP

Best Innovators adjust their innovation machines all the time, seeking the right balance of short- versus long-term projects, new products, and incremental improvement. They are specific about innovation speed—the pace of an idea's development and commercialization—and they're attuned to measures of how long it takes for an idea to develop into a money-making product. They draw an *innovation roadmap* to get them where they say they need to go.

Among the rewards of this rigorous setting of coordinates are the guidelines a company creates for weaving innovation strategy into everything it does, reinforcing the foundation of culture and process. Search fields are the earliest stage of an idea's evolution and necessarily very broadly defined. But they still need to be defined, even broadly, and the definition is something that every Best Innovator has to frame for itself.

Tata Motors developed its search fields with the intention of raising its profile in the small-car segment of India's auto industry. For Volkswagen (German Best Innovator, 2008), the search fields are not only complex but also broad, which is appropriate for a global giant producing multiple product lines.

In each case—Tata, Volkswagen, and every Best Innovator—the search-field portfolio is a ferment of insights drawn from hearing the voice of the customer, from applied industry knowledge of technology and competitors, and from watching the wide horizon of scientific, social, and political trends of all kinds. A firefighting-equipment maker might study ways to make its products more comfortable for women (Rosenbauer, Austria Best Innovator, 2009). A home-products company might take note of how bathrooms are emerging as a surprising status signifier in the West and, increasingly, elsewhere (Henkel Laundry & Home Care, German Best Innovator, 2010).

The search-field portfolio is the starting point of the innovation roadmap, which ideally looks ahead to the eventual end of an innovation's life cycle. Especially striking about Best Innovators is how many are thinking about a product's whole life cycle, including not just future improvements but its inevitable eclipse by the next big idea.

"In line with Schumpeter's theory of creative destruction, innovation can also include the decision to leave behind some areas of the present business," says Georg Kapsch, CEO of Kapsch TrafficCom (Best Innovator, 2008). "It is not only about doing new things but also about getting rid of traditional products, services, and even companies. Otherwise, we could not afford to invest in new areas."

The roadmap keeps the organization on track, describing not only budget and personnel but also *when* an innovation will enter the market and begin to earn back its investment—its time to market and time to profit.

ALIGNMENT IN SUPPORT OF THE INNOVATION PORTFOLIO

For Best Innovators, the job of prioritizing the possibilities in their innovation portfolios is never finished. At every point along the way to market, the business case for an idea is tested to see if it still holds up.

This would seem to be an obvious best practice for any company, and yet it is frequently overlooked, usually because of poor communication norms. Markets move, planning premises change, and variability in the cost of raw materials alters pricing dynamics even before a product launches. All of these have direct effects on profitability. A regular *update of planning premises* is an institutional habit with Best Innovators. A change in those premises might mean one idea needs to be killed or delayed while another is brought forward in the portfolio's list of priorities.

An innovation portfolio is like a funnel. But the Best Innovator funnel has an odd shape. It does not taper steadily to product launch. Instead, the funnel abruptly pinches near the middle, around the time search fields begin to yield specific ideas that can be argued with a business case or, as the case may be, rejected.

An innovation portfolio is built on a sequence of stage gates shepherding ideas on their way to market. An idea that can be tested for its investment risk advances to the narrow part of the funnel: the development-project portfolio. At this point, a new service or product begins getting concrete in its features and value proposition. This is also the point at which it is either shelved or rejected.

At every stage in an idea's development, collaboration makes a concept stronger. The definition for collaboration is cross-functional cooperation within the organization. We find this sort of internal alignment typical of Best Innovators, but—sometimes to our surprise—it is not always the norm among their peers.

"The dilemma," Kapsch observes, "is how to establish some form of organizational ambidexterity." By ambidexterity, he means being an organization of multiple competencies. Many CEOs would agree—in theory. But the practice is more difficult.

Internal alignment is a predictor for an innovation's long-term value to a company and its shareholders. We all know, for example, about Sony's failure in the mobile entertainment market. Often forgotten is that senior leadership didn't focus the attention of the whole organization on the meaning of mobile entertainment for growth. Eventually, the consequence was the surrender of Sony's early lead in smartphones and Apple's dominance of the market.

"Cross-functional" does not mean that an idea is developed sequentially, handed along from function to function for each to give their particular perspective. Time and again we've seen exactly that process, and time and again we've seen it add layers of unnecessary cost and complexity that reduce profitability by eye-popping amounts, as we will see in chapter 5, "Increase Innovation Efficiency and Speed." A cross-functional approach is a collective effort, a genuine collaboration with diverse elements of a company learning from one another and working toward a single vision.

In running their innovation-strategy processes, many companies struggle to define the balance of top-down guidance from senior management versus bottom-up participation by the grassroots of the organization. Best Innovators think past this hierarchical conundrum by thinking cross-functionally. Henkel did it by creating what it calls InnoPower teams, responsible for specific product categories and all related innovation projects. The teams develop innovation strategies (in consultation with senior management), which are then approved in Henkel's annual planning process and then implemented. The teams are chaired by a product-category leader and include representatives from every major function. Participating in InnoPower teams is a mandatory step on the career path of Henkel's high-potential employees.

Best Innovators have all kinds of organizational structures, but overall, they integrate more internal functions in the innovation process than the average of all participants in the competition. All of them have well-considered processes to ensure continuous cross-functional involvement of pivotal internal functions—chief among them R&D, production, sales, and tellingly, procurement.

The talent for cross-functional collaboration is true of Best Innovators when they engage in partnerships outside their own organizations. Best Innovators know that the best and brightest talents don't all work for them. To supplement their inventory of competencies, Best Innovators appear to step naturally into intimate collaborative relationships with an array of outside players—from customers and suppliers to universities, government agencies, and even competitors.

The world is a complex place, after all, with knowledge generated from every corner. Best Innovators see the world as a network of knowledge clusters, of which their organization is just one. For Best Innovators, knowledge management is more than a vogue phrase. It is an actively managed capability in support of alignment and creative flexibility. Best Innovators link their cluster to others, transfusing capabilities into—and across—their organizations. Coca-Cola, for instance, has built a process for scouting the world for the technical competencies it needs to support innovation. It calls the process External Technology Assessment/Acquisition.

"You basically plug yourself into the nerve center of science, research, innovation, and entrepreneurship outside the company and around the world," says Guy Wollaert, Coke's CTO. "We have a map called the heat map of technology and invention, and we deliberately plug ourselves into those nerve centers. I call it 'plug the brain.'"

As a group, Best Innovators are consistent in their concern for the distribution of new thinking, especially new thinking that emerges from successful initiatives in one part of the company but that might have application in another part. This is what Volkswagen CTO Ulrich Hackenberg calls "democratizing innovation."

But what does this kind of flexibility look like in an organization that also wants to be rigorous in its management process? A fair amount of the time, it looks like managed tension.

The tension is managed with clear guidance about developing innovation strategy—the things people in an organization should be thinking about—without being overly prescriptive, like Whirlpool has done, to cite just one example.

The KPIs to which Best Innovators are conspicuously attached help enormously in providing guidance. They let senior managers and members of an organization at large track the progress of the innovation portfolio with hard facts. When speaking to the senior leaders of Best Innovator winners, it is remarkable how many can rattle off KPIs for their innovation strategies, especially NPVI, time to market, and even time to profit—the latter a measure of how long a product needs to become profitable, measured from the moment it was decided to develop the product or service. It is the essential KPI of an innovation portfolio.

That clarity is essential to providing a creative structure to the overlapping networks we've described. Members of those networks—not all of them inside the organization—need to communicate with one another and make decisions quickly. With one collaboration tool or another, they talk to each other (which we acknowledge is unnerving to many IT departments). Most of these conversations about commercializing ideas are not explicitly directed by senior management. But with clarity of vision and agreement on mission, the collective evaluation of ideas acquires structure that permits new ideas to be applied faster.

THE STRUCTURE OF AN INNOVATIVE ORGANIZATION

What organizational structure supports innovation? There is no single correct structure. Best Innovators are pragmatists that find rigor in their processes and design an organization that supports them. However, certain themes repeat. Best Innovators all build direct links between innovation initiatives and C-level executives. If organizational culture is shaped by what is prized, then commitment to innovation is shaped by the behavior of senior leaders. If leaders don't spend time cherishing their innovators, they will not channel the company's energy in the right direction.

Best Innovators address innovation management "from the market to the market" and manipulate five areas to improve their innovation performance and propel sustainable and profitable growth (see figure 3). In this book, chapter by chapter, we take you through the five areas, discussing each in great detail.

Figure 3

The Masters of Innovation focus on five innovation management areas—*from* the market *to* the market

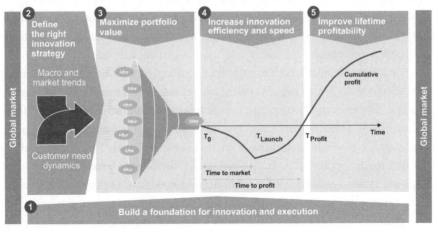

Source: A.T. Kearney

In chapter 2, we talk about building the foundations of an innovative organization. This is about developing a culture and mindset that is open to innovation and putting the right processes and governance structures in place to master the innovation challenges. Best Innovators nurture their innovation culture by shaping the environment, mindset, and way of working. They shape the world before if shapes them, even if it means taking on a difficult transformation. More specifically, it is about creating an innovation culture, cultivating an entrepreneurial mindset, encouraging appropriate risks, finding inspiration everywhere, and committing to repeatable processes.

Chapter 3 is all about doing the early work of innovation strategy. Innovation begins with analyzing relevant technology, market trends, and customer needs to understand the potential challenges and opportunities as input for defining an "actionable" innovation strategy. Best Innovators link their understanding of market and technology dynamics to a broadly agreed-upon search-field portfolio to steer idea generation. This entails knowing what you want to achieve, owning a point of view about the future, defining the innovation search fields, managing to the customer's desired outcome, knowing your own competencies and investing accordingly, and drawing the innovation roadmap.

Chapter 4, "Maximize Portfolio Value," is about generating as many ideas as possible for the innovation search fields and then applying the right evaluation criteria to quickly select and flesh out the most promising ideas. In this way, limited resources are allocated effectively. Best Innovators have better processes in place to involve a broad range of stakeholders in generating ideas to fuel the idea portfolio, and they involve the most knowledgeable internal and external experts to make fast decisions about which ideas to pursue. This implies managing your innovation portfolio holistically, pursuing truly open innovation, and boosting the transfer success rate.

In chapter 5, we turn to innovation speed and efficiency. This means bringing the newly developed product or service to market as fast and cost-efficiently as possible. This is essential to optimize profitable growth over the entire life cycle. To do so, Best Innovators work cross-functionally, manage innovation more consistently, and leverage the innovative power of their supply base. More specifically, it is about reducing time to profit, managing the big metrics, treating interoperability as a decisive capability, and collaborating early with the right suppliers.

Chapter 6 focuses on securing and increasing profitability over the life cycle of a product or service. Best Innovators leverage their innovation process excellence and their growing ideas network to make this a reality. Here we discuss the importance of a coherent process, managing complexity, working within agile and lean design, and further building and improving collaborative partnerships.

Finally, in chapter 7, we address the importance of durability—how the leaders are able to maintain their innovative concepts year after year. Substantial growth comes from delivering on durable innovation strategies, durable in their constancy and durable in their structured openness to change. This is, once again, a tension that Best Innovators manage well because they take great care in building their leadership teams.

Now, let's take a deeper look at how Best Innovators achieve their status and how they hold on to it year after year. We hope you enjoy the read!

THE FERRARI BRAND

Any company that says the first pillar of its innovation strategy is Formula 1 racing is going to attract attention. What makes a Ferrari one of the most sought-after automobiles in the world are the company's two other innovation pillars: brand and product.

"It's a self-fostering virtuous cycle," says Roberto Fedeli, senior vice president of Ferrari R&D. "Clients will always expect innovation in a new Ferrari. Without innovation, the product pillar goes down in terms of sales. Without innovation, we die."

The core value of Ferrari's innovation strategy is simple: the buyer's experience of the product, first and foremost.

"We sell emotions," Fedeli says. "All our innovations target that. To increase the driving experience, drivers must *feel* the innovation."

That places an emphasis on what Fedeli calls "know-how transfer from Formula 1." It also stresses time to market, the speed with which Ferrari brings innovation to drivers. It marries know-how from its Formula 1 program with research already launched and already generating preliminary results, often drawing on research from other industries.

"The objective is to bring knowledge 'on road' as soon as possible," Fedeli says. "We are determined to bring an innovation from idea to the product within one to two years. This is possible only by aligning our innovation program with our cycle plan and defining which will be the first product to first use an innovation."

This requires a complex operating model. Ferrari's processes, Fedeli says, are "well-defined, although not formalized, based on flexibility. We never freeze decisions or solutions until the very end of the process." Consistency with product architecture and time to market is ensured by a hybrid organization balanced between research and development functions and project teams, which stay current with open options and new components in development.

"If there is an issue with a solution, it does not impact the product," he says, "because we always have an alternative, a backup solution. We don't have a benchmark. We are the frontline of sports car innovation. This is a differentiating aspect with respect to followers. It's culturally different."

STMICROELECTRONICS' MERCILESSLY SHORT INNOVATION LIFE CYCLE

STMicroelectronics is the largest semiconductor company in Europe. Its innovation strategy is driven by two powerful facts: even at $8 billion annually, it competes against a wide range of companies in North America and Asia, some of which are much larger. And it competes in markets that are well-established (automobiles, computers and IT infrastructure, set-top boxes, and mobile phones), recent (sports- and fitness-related applications), and even nascent (medical applications). In all of its markets, the innovation life cycle is mercilessly short. Perpetual innovation is ST's only competitive choice.

ST knows that succeeding at its innovation strategy is beyond the scope of what it can do alone. When the company received the 2007 Best Innovator award in France, senior managers attributed ST's success to "a common work culture with all the players throughout our value chain, from research laboratories to suppliers, manufacturers, customers, as well as competitors."

ST was formed out of the 1987 merger of Italy's SGS Microelettronica and France's Thomson Semiconducteurs. From its earliest years, ST tied the execution of its innovation strategy to long-term partnerships with key customers and suppliers, leading universities and research institutes, and even competitors. Today, almost 20 percent of its employees work in R&D and product design in one of the company's 10 advanced R&D centers across the globe.

ST has also been involved in key European R&D collaborative efforts, including the intergovernmental organization EUREKA and two public-private partnerships: the European Nanoelectronics Initiative Advisory Council (ENIAC) and Electronic Components and Systems for European Leadership (ECSEL).

"While costs for the industry were rising sky high," says Jean-Marc Chery, ST's chief operating officer, "our deep-rooted culture of cooperation in R&D programs has enabled us to remain one of the leaders in technology process development and manufacturing in the industry."

MEET WHIRLPOOL BRAZIL

Whirlpool Corporation is a $19 billion appliance maker. Headquartered in Michigan, Whirlpool's products are sold in nearly every country on earth. More than a quarter of its worldwide revenue comes from its Latin American operation.

As an organization, Whirlpool is distinguished by attention to key performance indicators. The performance of every business unit head, for example, is measured against an expectation that 25 percent of a division's sales will come from recent innovations. In Latin America, that includes several products from Brastemp, the leading appliance brand in Brazil. Among Brastemp's innovations is the Smart Cook, the first stove to connect to smartphones, and its Ative washing machines that calculate the weight of the clothes and automatically measure soap and fabric softener.

Whirlpool Latin America is run from São Paulo. Among the observations of the Best

Innovator judges in 2010, the year Whirlpool won its Best Innovator award, was that Brazilian companies are becoming steadily more international in the way they conceptualize innovation.

Whirlpool, for example, runs four technology centers in Brazil, each focused on one of the company's core product groups: refrigeration, laundry, cooking, and air conditioning. These are in addition to three manufacturing plants. According to Brazil's National Institute of Industrial Property, Whirlpool is the fourth-largest patent holder in the country.[3] Of its 14,500 employees in Brazil, 700 are exclusively dedicated to Whirlpool's product research and development.

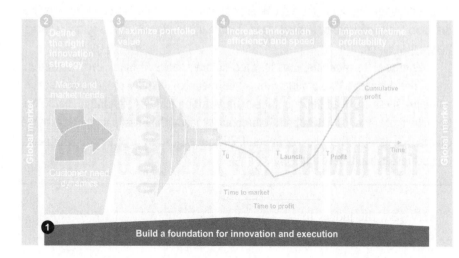

CHAPTER 2

BUILD THE FOUNDATION
FOR INNOVATION AND EXECUTION

Every year, the judges for the Best Innovator competition screen dozens of entries from around the world. Reading them is an illuminating exercise. When we ask entrants if they would characterize their organizations as having a culture of innovation and process excellence, almost all say "Yes!" However, operational results may tell a very different story.

For example, most entrants describe the structure of their organizations in very similar terms. Most look quite conventional. This tells us that the difference between the winners and everyone else is not a direct consequence of organizational design (no matter what you may have read to the contrary). And it demonstrates that the habit of innovation is not the consequence of organizational design all by itself. The architecture of an innovative organization cannot be described with a chart of where everyone sits.

What *is* characteristic of the Best Innovators is the active management of innovation. This chapter shares the lessons we've learned from Best Innovators about building the foundation of an innovative organization.

- **Create an innovation culture.** Best Innovators are serious about innovation culture. Culture is the sum of what is prized by an organization. To build culture, Best Innovators create an environment where entrepreneurial people thrive.

- **Cultivate an entrepreneurial mindset.** Best Innovators nourish freedom to spark creativity and, quite consistently, new business. With independence and entrepreneurialism comes risk, and that risk needs to be managed.

- **Encourage appropriate risks.** Best Innovators communicate to their organization an acceptable risk profile by describing it in relation to the future. In an innovative organization, taking a risk and losing are not obstacles to career advancement.

- **Find inspiration everywhere.** Best Innovators have let go of their faith in eureka moments. The essential condition of innovation is collaboration across functions and across geographies.

- **Commit to repeatable processes.** Best Innovators make process management—the facts—the active center of their innovation culture. Facts are the underpinning of a convincing argument for a common vision, heightening the emotions of an innovation culture.

CREATE AN INNOVATION CULTURE

One habit that distinguishes Best Innovators is the balancing of emotion and fact—their obvious commitment to innovation culture and process excellence. Active management of this balance needs to be visible to business-unit heads and ultimately to the chief executive officer. How senior leaders respond to the innovators in their organization tells their team—as well as analysts and investors—most of what they need to know about the seriousness of the company's commitment to innovation.

A balanced foundation of emotion and fact—of culture and process—creates the conditions for making innovation repeatable and efficient. Most entrants in the Best Innovator competition—the winners and the rest—give themselves high marks for both fact *and* emotion. Consider, for instance, the typical responses to the culture questions: is your organization excited about innovation? Genuinely open to new ideas? Ready for change? Check, check, and check. But we often see something different when we get past this self-assessment to a rigorous observation of the organization in action.

It is revealing, for example, that when we visit a company that declares its passion for innovation, we frequently find that neither the CEO nor anyone else with a C-suite title is available to talk about how much innovation matters. In German, this is known as *Selbstbetrug*—self-deception. This is exactly the sort of signal that even the farthest-flung members of an organization are adept at reading. If the first element of innovation culture is the behavior of senior leadership—and it certainly is—then innovation's centrality must be visible all the time, starting with the CEO's calendar.

All of us can tell stories of self-deception in organizations that say they are committed to innovation. Compare that with the sound of authentically committed leadership from several of the Best Innovators:

"If I choose a path, I follow it until the end, and nothing will stop me."
Jan Musil, CEO and chairman, ČKD

"It is vital to establish a brand identified with innovation that leads customers to continuously choose us as their partner. I want customers to feel we are indispensable to their business."
Tetsuji Ohashi, president and CEO, Komatsu

"The CEO is the major advertisement for innovation. The CEO inspires people to continue their collaborative creativity without worrying about not being recognized if an idea does not move forward. The CEO creates a culture of encouraging people to minimize their own mental blocks."
Abel Rochinha, CEO, Coelce

No one would argue against the primacy of culture in creating a consistently innovative organization. After all, every well-known book about innovation tells us this is true. But what *is* culture? And how do the Best Innovators build it?

CULTURE IS THE SUM OF WHAT IS PRIZED

What is an innovative culture? Drawing on the experience of the Best Innovator competition, we define culture as the shared values and behavior norms that guide not just what people do but *how* they do it.

Culture is the often-unspoken consensus about where energy flows. It is the unwritten rulebook for "the way we do things around here." Because its negatives are unspoken, a malformed culture is a damaging force, a retardant to innovation. Consciously managed and actively guided, however, culture can be the foundation of sustained innovation.

Consider 3M, a giant among the world's innovators. Headquartered in St. Paul, Minnesota, 3M manufactures nearly 60,000 products found in hospitals, offices, homes, and industries around the globe.

3M boasts a 112-year history of invention. Yet today, one-third of its revenue comes from products that are less than five years old. CEO Inge Thulin is

BUILDING AN INNOVATION CULTURE: THE ELEMENTS YOU HAVE TO GET RIGHT

ENVIRONMENT	**Values:** Innovation is embedded in the operational principles. **Leadership:** Managers' behavior supports innovation and demonstrates that innovation is a priority. **Recognition:** Innovations and innovators are recognized and rewarded. **Freedom:** The company gives employees time and space for innovation.
MINDSET	**Creativity:** Employees are open to new ideas and solve problems imaginatively. **Risk taking:** Taking appropriate risks is fostered, and failures are learned from rather than punished. **Customer orientation:** Delighting the customer through innovation and quality is a demonstrated obsession.
WAYS OF WORKING	**Collaboration**: Cooperation defines work that takes place across functions and across locations. **Ownership:** Innovation is everyone's job and can come from anywhere, within or outside the organization and its networks. **Openness:** The company inoculates against "not-invented-here" syndrome. There is openness to and acceptance of external ideas and partners.

aiming to raise that to 37 percent by 2017.

How does a company with more than a century of innovation in its past continue to evolve in the future? That was the challenge faced by Thulin in 2012, when he assumed leadership of 3M. He was a 30-year veteran of the company and thoroughly versed in its culture. In his first days as CEO, he and his team laid out a vision for 3M: technology advancing every company, products enhancing every home, and innovation improving every life.

Six core business strategies coupled with three strategic levers—which have investment in innovation at their core—support 3M's vision and enhance its competitiveness. Thulin's particular focus has been on Class 4 and 5 products, those that are new to existing markets or new to entirely new markets. He calls these "disruptive game-changing technologies."

"One of the ways we accomplish this is that we do R&D a bit differently— we separate the R and the D," Thulin says. "The scientists in our central research facility are free to focus on pure research, looking for unexpected, unscripted opportunities for breakthroughs. 3M's development teams in each of our business groups then draw upon the technologies developed by central research. No single business within 3M is the owner of these technologies."

Collaboration is another core value 3M believes is crucial to igniting innovation. This includes working closely both with customers and among its own employees. The goal is to ensure inventions have practical applications in the marketplace. For example, admission to 3M's prestigious Carlton Society, which honors the company's best scientists, is based both on scientific prowess and commitment to mentoring.

3M's spirit of collaboration extends to its 46 core technology platforms, which range from adhesives and abrasives to sensors and electronics materials. This technology pool is shared by scientists from all five business groups and from all of 3M's corporate laboratories, which are located in 35 countries.

That's how a homogenous mixing technology originally created for dental work made its way into automotive applications, too, leading to successful products and well-served customers.

3M's culture of innovation and collaboration can be traced back to William L. McKnight, who joined 3M as a bookkeeper in 1907 when it was still known as the Minnesota Mining & Manufacturing Company. McKnight rose to chairman, ultimately serving the company for nearly 60 years. Today, 3M's culture remains rooted in McKnight's values.

Even if you're not fortunate enough to inherit a culture of innovation, one can be built—even in resistant circumstances.

Consider Coelce, the power company that won Best Innovator in 2012 and 2013. Coelce operates in the northeastern region of Brazil under a contract with the national government. At first, the organization saw little point in senior management's efforts to promote innovation. What could the reward be? A push to create a culture of innovation that began inside Coelce in 2000 was initially resisted as bureaucratic sloganeering—a make-work project.

But over the past 15 years, Coelce has built the foundation for a culture of innovation with a persistence of vision. Over time, this has come to engage all levels of the organization and positioned the utility for growth in a region that has lately seen accelerated growth.

"Innovation has helped us increase employee satisfaction and improve process efficiency," says CEO Abel Rochinha. "No one knows the processes better than the ones involved in daily operations. Employees feel committed and accountable since they feel they have the power to make things change and that they're valued for that."

For clothing retailer Desigual, a culture that is open to innovation is essential. "Innovation is as key to the history of Desigual as it is to its future," says CEO Manel Jadraque. "We innovate in every way. In product design, our garments are 100 percent unequaled." (Desigual is the Spanish word for unequal.) The key to the firm's success, he says, is a combination of small things well done. "But what makes a real difference is our boldness, our attitude to risk thinking and creating each category, each collection, and each product," he says. "We promote creativity with a premise that there is neither fear nor blame."

Each collection starts with more than 5,000 ideas, half of which are selected in the first phase, which is then narrowed down to the 10 percent that reaches stores. "We believe this is the basis of the innovation that allows us to achieve sustainable and profitable growth along our path," Jadraque adds.

CULTIVATE AN ENTREPRENEURIAL MINDSET

In 1948, 3M's McKnight set down his basic rule of management. Embedded in three short paragraphs—not much more than a note to himself—is a broad philosophy of innovation culture that creates an environment where smart people can thrive. "Management that is destructively critical when mistakes are made kills initiative," McKnight said. "And it's essential that we have many people with initiative if we are to continue to grow."

It was McKnight who, more than six decades ago, encouraged 3M employees to spend 15 percent of their work time on their own projects and ideas. That initiative is still alive and well today and has led to some of 3M's most well-known products.

Naturally, we would like to presume that leadership is always committed to innovation. But our experience tells us that reality is, to put it politely, more complex. Senior managers and unit heads are necessarily protective of the near-term health of their core business. In fact, most senior managers are evaluated on the performance of the core business from quarter to quarter. The difficulty is in sticking with the often long lead times required to nurture a new idea into a business without slighting the responsibility to next quarter's targets or the interests of shareholders.

We never said it was easy.

"Day-to-day work is not counterproductive or somehow poison for innovation," says Peer M. Schatz, CEO of QIAGEN, the global maker of diagnostic and life-science technologies that won the 2011 Best Innovator competition. On the contrary, Schatz says, the daily demands of a business are catalytic to a culture of innovation.

"The cultural element is by far the most important success factor for innovation," he says. "But it requires an expectation that innovation is part of everyday life and not separate from it."

The leadership style Schatz describes is a cultural value. Leaders who consistently support innovation make it a visible priority. They model it both for employees and for external communities, including suppliers, partners and, of course, the analysts and shareholders accustomed to living quarter to quarter. For all, the point is the same: the commitment must be obvious and persistent.

The foundation of an innovation culture is about more than just sending signals. There needs to be substance, concrete and plain to see across the organization—for example, with KPIs such as 3M's NPVI that call out the percentage of revenue from new products. In chapter 4, "Maximize Portfolio Value," we look closely at best practices in the development of KPIs for innovation. But there is another measure of commitment to innovation just as tangible as NPVI in cultural terms: programmatic recognition for innovators.

Best Innovators offer a range of approaches to recognize innovation. Some award a medal or a bonus. Some include contribution to innovation as part of every performance evaluation. Others are splashier and more public. For example, the Best Innovator awards are presented at an Innovator Recognition Ceremony attended by more than 1,000 people. A longtime corporate innovator, 3M also created a recognition called the Carlton Society, which grants membership to employees who not only demonstrate technical excellence but also actively share it. QIAGEN holds similar recognition ceremonies.

Compensation counts as recognition too. Never forget that. But for the best and brightest, recognition counts at least as much—or it should. To fill an organization's talent pipeline with those sorts of talents, a demonstrated commitment to innovation should be part of the hiring criteria.

Best Innovators encourage freedom to innovate across the organization. QIAGEN, for instance, has what Schatz describes as an open-door policy. "Exchanges with decision makers and our executive committee are explicitly requested," he says. "Every employee gets the chance to present themselves and their good ideas in front of top management." QIAGEN presses senior executives to transfer responsibilities and create room for autonomy at every level. It is a tactic deliberately intended to recruit every employee into a learning culture, with all that can mean for new business and new growth.

"You want employees to say all is not just a big machine called 'status quo' that cannot be changed," says Schatz, "but that there's the possibility of offering better approaches. The organizational policies have to make room for creativity, and leadership has to demonstrate that innovation is part of day-to-day business."

Firefighting-equipment maker Rosenbauer International AG does something similar. The company initiates "impulse rounds" to solve specific development tasks—to collect the requirements, say, to create a new firefighting vehicle or a pump technology. Impulse rounds bring together different departments and create a forum for cross-functional associations and free discussion. The results are often striking in their contribution to rapid prototyping, says CTO Gottfried Brunbauer, but the longer-term impact may be on reaffirming Rosenbauer's open culture. The long-term point of nurturing such freedom is the hope of sparking creativity and, one hopes, new business.

This is explicit at Rational AG, the German manufacturer of combi steamers for commercial kitchens. Rational won the 2008 Best Innovator award for small- and medium-size enterprises and was the overall winner in 2012. "Every employee is encouraged to be an independent entrepreneur," says former chairman and CEO Günter Blaschke. "They're expected to independently manage their tasks, optimize their work methods, make decisions, and take responsibility."

Rational employees put their name on every oven they build to underscore the individual sense of ownership. Blaschke is convinced that the effect of such practices has been to nurture a mindset that assumes openness to new ideas and inspires creative solutions to problems.

Managers see themselves as first among equals and engage with employees on what Blaschke calls "eye level." They encourage freedom to think out loud and to create the optimum climate for individual professional development. The progress Rational has made in fostering this business approach can be seen in the fact that 93 percent of all employees report being not just satisfied but proud to work for the company.

Blaschke knows the organization is always watching. "How we handle new ideas from colleagues has a lasting impact," he says, "not just on the immediate idea but on their willingness to generate ideas in the future."

ENCOURAGE APPROPRIATE RISKS

With independence and entrepreneurialism comes risk, and that risk needs to be managed. As William McKnight once remarked, "Mistakes will be made. But if a person is essentially right, the mistakes he or she makes are not as serious in the long run as the mistakes management will make if it undertakes to tell those in authority exactly how they must do their jobs."

The difficulty for any organization, as for any entrepreneur, lies in knowing how to define appropriate risk.

The best-selling books about innovation assert that failure must be learned from, not punished. But what does it mean to have a failure-friendly innovation culture—one in which even bizarre ideas get a fair hearing? It's one thing to say "learn from failure" and quite another to stay cool when failure happens. Best Innovators demonstrate exactly that kind of cool.

Since 2003 when the Best Innovator competition began, we've noticed that in a consistently innovative organization, taking a risk and losing is not an obstacle to career advancement. In fact, Tata Group showcases failures—and the teams behind them—for the instruction that misfires provide. In 2010 and 2011, for example, fewer than half of 3,200 would-be innovations generated by Tata's 80 companies achieved any commercial success. In the auto group, an unconventional transmission that could not meet the targeted performance had to be dropped, and a proposed new door panel for its small car, the Nano, didn't meet cost targets. But Tata spotlighted both of these failures as an encouragement to audacity.[4]

Failures are a test for innovation culture. No project should be kept on life support for fear of punishment or of looking stupid. But sometimes, the plug must be pulled to avoid throwing good money after bad.

Kapsch TrafficCom, one of Austria's leading technology companies and a

2008 Best Innovator, follows a cultural path similar to Tata's. The company knows that sometimes even an interesting idea needs to be stopped in development.

"Experience shows that the way we deal with failure is critical," says CEO Georg Kapsch. "It's important to celebrate what I call successful failures: projects that go the wrong way but get stopped in time. An employee or manager who has the courage to do that is officially recognized." He argues that "managed failures" are successes because of the learning opportunities they offer, which he contends "helps develop the trial-and-error culture vital to venturing."

FIND INSPIRATION EVERYWHERE

One answer to the question of weighing new ideas that seems to come almost instinctively to Best Innovators is "design thinking." Our former colleague Harsh Jawharkar describes design thinking as an outside-in approach to invention and product development. At its heart lies customer orientation: the determination to delight customers through innovation and quality that borders on an organizational obsession. As Jawharkar points out, designers employ the classic observational techniques of ethnographers, studying customers in their "natural environments" and taking detailed notes about their interactions with a product or a service. A crucial part of this is encouraging customers to tell stories about their experience with a product—and then listening to what they have to say. This allows fast "failures" (we use the word ironically) through prototyping and early customer feedback.

"The primary factor of successful innovation is going to customers and learning from them on a daily basis," says Tetsuji Ohashi, president and CEO of Komatsu, the Japanese manufacturer of mining and construction equipment. "When people talk about customer needs, they usually mean customers as one group," he says. "But customers differ depending on where they work. Their needs, even when building a stretch of road, will change due to differences in country, say, or in the natural environment." For example, he points to several prominent Japanese construction firms that are struggling to build expressways in developing countries because what is required of an expressway in those places is very different from what is required in Japan.

With respect to customer insight, Rosenbauer, the Austrian manufacturer of firefighting equipment and 2009 Best Innovator for organization and culture, has an advantage. Many of its employees volunteer with local fire-service brigades in their free time and therefore end up using the company's products—in effect becoming Rosenbauer's customers. Gottfried Brunbauer, the company's

CTO who has charge of its innovation efforts, observes that being volunteer firefighters "ensures a multitude of ideas and makes the innovation process very efficient. In the person of our own employees, we directly incorporate our customers in the innovation process."

Once organizations let go of their faith in eureka moments, the essential condition of innovation becomes collaboration. Collaboration is not just what happens between people who happen to work near each other. It takes place across functions and across locations—and often not in person. To make it all coherent, the Best Innovators typically have a foundation of stringent controls, focused on planning assumptions to avoid surprises later.

Many of the Best Innovators say innovation is everyone's job, and it can come from anywhere. That's great, but this rich ferment must be managed. It must be actively coordinated under the eye of senior management, whoever that might be—the business-unit head, the CIO, the head of R&D, or the CTO. At all phases of the innovation process, any combination of internal capabilities—marketing, sales, R&D, sourcing, after-sales—is possible.

3M uses a networked approach. Since 1951, it has held technical forums where all research and development personnel share what they're working on with colleagues whom they might not otherwise ever meet.

Or consider the challenge at QIAGEN, which has actively worked to balance what can feel like tension between a lively innovation culture and structured processes. Pursuing a perpetually recharged stream of ideas for its innovation portfolio, QIAGEN makes an active choice to push the boundaries of its operating culture. In addition to supporting employees in a constant questioning of organizational behaviors, QIAGEN explores new ways to build its capacity to see beyond the horizon.

One such experiment was what the company used to call its Beyond! process, during which QIAGEN assigned several teams to ad hoc think tanks. The teams were challenged to balance creativity and hard facts. They collected ideas, filtered them, and then suggested the most promising ones as development projects. This sounds ideal, but QIAGEN realized that innovation was being seen as a world of its own without much contact with day-to-day business.

"Innovation is not an island," says Schatz. "It has its sources across the whole company, and the drive toward innovation can't be dogmatically pressed into systems. Many different influences affect innovation success, from serendipity to structured processes." Not that QIAGEN wasn't systematic in the development of its innovation portfolio, he adds, but it was evident that the Beyond! process "did not match well with our processes."

Today, innovation is integrated into QIAGEN's daily business. Schatz says this gives the company an up-close view of customers, first of all, as well as suppliers and others QIAGEN regards as stakeholders in its innovation strategy. Schatz is well aware of all the company owes to this integrated approach to building its innovation portfolio.

An ironic challenge for managers of the innovation process is balancing a strong sense of ownership with openness to fresh thinking that may come from somewhere else—in other words, from the outside in. We all have experience with the "not-invented-here" syndrome—the often unacknowledged resistance to good ideas tainted either by their origin or by their challenge to the core business. This is a reflex unsuited to a networked world in which any number of external collaborators may also be profitably involved in managing innovation, from idea generation to product development to launch.

These external collaborations include suppliers, universities, and consultants with various kinds of expertise, even in some cases competitors. But they begin with implicit collaborations with customers. In the chapters "Define the Right Innovation Strategy" and "Maximize Portfolio Value," we work through such customer collaborations in detail. In both of these levers, the foundation of success begins with a *customer orientation* that needs to be second nature.

The Best Innovators integrate more internal and external functions in their innovation management than the average participants in the competition. The winners are distinguished by something else too: they have processes in place to make sure they know where they are on their innovation journeys.

COMMIT TO REPEATABLE PROCESSES

If innovation isn't to be a forlorn bet on eureka moments and is instead to be a managed, repeatable process, then process management—the facts—must be an active part of the foundation. To make the right strategic choices, managers and their organizations need to have the facts.

By facts, we mean the processes that guide an idea from insight to concept to launch to its eventual eclipse by subsequent innovations—in other words, an innovation's life cycle. From its birth to its old age, an innovation is measured by progress tracking, deviation analysis, coordination of innovation, and results from functional strategies. These are fact-driven processes. They might not capture the passions of people who might be inspired to innovate, but they are the underpinning of a convincing argument for a common vision, heightening the emotions of innovation culture.

No set of process controls should be so rigid that they prevent eureka moments. But the world is volatile. It would be reckless not to have well-constructed volatility controls in place as a commercial idea evolves.

This is especially true for innovation projects with long lead times. Exposure to volatility may matter more to some industries than others—less to pharmaceuticals, say, for which most costs are in research and development, and more to manufacturers vulnerable to price swings in raw materials. For example, in our consulting work, we saw one manufacturer develop a business case for a great new product. But over the course of its development, the product sponsors didn't update the business case, which is to say they didn't manage their planning premises. Three years later, the product was launched with disappointing profitability because the price of raw materials had gone up.

Bear in mind that process management is not a two-dimensional task of getting a single idea from one end of a pipeline to the other. It is the end-to-end management of multiple ideas at individual stages of their life cycles, each in its own way part of the organization's overall innovation portfolio. That makes managing the facts challenging—and essential.

Characteristic of all Best Innovators is clear assignment of management responsibility for guiding an idea from infancy to the day it becomes a business reality. Where innovation-management jobs sit within a company is subject to any number of organizational designs, although typically there is one for each business unit or division. The job of the innovation manager is not dreaming up new ideas, necessarily, but steering their progress toward commercialization.

"Just as free cash flow is the blood of the company organism, innovation and constant improvement are its oxygen," says ČKD Group CEO Jan Musil. "Therefore, anyone can come up with ideas for innovation." ČKD, the Czech company that won a 2012 Best Innovator award, is a privately held association of engineering and production companies focused on engineering, procurement, and construction for a range of energy industries, including power, oil and gas, renewables, environmental technology, and infrastructure development.

"Our innovation processes," Musil says, "are pretty typical project-management processes. Right from the beginning, each project sets up a system for test-data management, for example. In parallel, the best business strategy and best client for the pilot installation are being sought."

Henkel's Laundry & Home Care business unit, an overall Best Innovator winner in 2009/2010, also focuses its attention on the balance between clear global processes and those involving personnel in and around its headquarters as part of its "glocal" strategy. Executive vice president Bruno Piacenza describes the company's processes as "open but controlled" with clear lines of responsibilities. It seems to be working: in 2013, Laundry & Home Care increased its innovation rate—the percentage share of sales generated with products younger than three years—to 45 percent. The goal is to raise that to 50 percent in the near future.

The kind of progress tracking and coordination of innovation and functional strategies at which ČKD and Henkel excel is characteristic of Best Innovators. Tellingly, among all the elements of progress tracking, Best Innovator applicants—the winners and everyone else—have had to work hardest to master the challenges of deviation analysis, the control of planning premises, and the control of planning processes.

What distinguishes the winners is that they build a foundation for innovation—and then they keep on building it. The reward is a transparent view into the progress of their organizations—into the facts.

Best Innovators are good at balancing *both* emotion and fact, culture and process—not just one or the other in some right-brained, left-brained dichotomy. This ambidexterity is foundational to their capacity for making innovation repeatable and efficient. In good times and in lean times, Best Innovators are consistent in this commitment.

Best Innovators make clear what their organizations prize—through the behavior of their leadership, their tolerance for risk (and honorable failure), and the public celebration of innovation and entrepreneurialism within their own ranks. Their organizational values are noticeably enduring, surviving leadership changes and the passing of years.

Best Innovators find inspiration everywhere. They find it first in the voice of the customer, of course, but they are also active listeners to talented voices across their organizations. They take it for granted that good ideas are bubbling up all around them. What distinguishes them from their peers is their success in channeling these good ideas in commercial directions with structured processes.

Best Innovators are loyal to their processes. Their processes yield the facts that guide innovation strategy, the facts that enable an organization to manage multiple possibilities—from their conception as market insights to their launch as money-making innovations.

This is an innovation life cycle. It is the evolution of a fertile innovation portfolio.

QIAGEN: EMPLOYEES ARE THE CENTER OF INNOVATION STRATEGY

In 2011, QIAGEN was the overall winner of the Best Innovator award. The company, which since its founding in 1984 has become a global leader in life sciences and molecular diagnostics, was cited for its innovative personnel processes, clear anchoring of innovation within the corporate culture, and a global innovation-management strategy. The Best Innovator competition's judges described all three as decisive to QIAGEN's success. The cumulative effect, the judges said, promoted inventive thinking among its 4,000 employees.

QIAGEN's competitors include household names in a variety of medical technologies. In more than a quarter century, the company has grown from a start-up to a world leader in molecular sample and assay technologies for molecular diagnostics, pharmaceutical companies, and academic research. QIAGEN is also a player in applied testing—forensics, food, and veterinary testing. In 2013, revenue was $1.3 billion.

QIAGEN's orientation toward proactivity created a culture of innovation, said the Best Innovator judges, who praised the company as a learning organization focused on inspiration, identity, and impact.

Peer Schatz, QIAGEN's chief executive officer, sees the company's competitive strength more simply.

"Our success factor," he says, "is that we place selection, development, and encouragement of employees at the center of our innovation management strategy." The most important things, he says, are not professional or functional expertise but certain character traits: courage and curiosity.

QIAGEN's innovation culture induces an openness to continual change and—when necessary—to radical transformation of the company's core value proposition. The company started off with chemistry, added biology to better understand customer applications, and then moved on to engineering to develop automated solutions for laboratory workflows. Most recently, the company has expanded into information technology, allowing users to analyze and interpret the enormous amount of data that new genomic sequencing technologies generate.

In addition to creating new infrastructures such as innovation labs or processes such as Beyond!, QIAGEN maintains strong relationships with leading academic research institutions (the traditional home turf for the company's life-science tools) to intensively work with creative scientific minds—an interaction Schatz says is an important source of new ideas and business inspirations.

SINGULAR FOCUS KEEPS RATIONAL AG ON TOP

Rational AG is an extraordinarily focused manufacturer of commercial cooking equipment. Even as it has developed subsidiaries in 19 countries in the past 40 years, the company continues to make a deliberate strategic choice to sustain a single core competency both for the depth of knowledge it can develop and for the closeness to customers it creates, says former chairman and CEO Günter Blaschke.

This focus earned Rational the Best Innovator award in 2013. The previous year was a rocky one in the European Union, and yet Rational increased revenue 11 percent to €435 million worldwide.

Headquartered in Landsberg am Lech in southern Germany, Rational holds a 54 percent share of the worldwide market for professional ovens. Since its founding in 1973, Rational has sold more than 600,000 appliances in more than 100 countries—each one built by an employee who stamped his or her name on it. Every day, 120 million meals are prepared with Rational cooking appliances.

CEWE STAYS AHEAD OF THE CURVE

For almost 40 years, CEWE was Europe's leading manufacturer of photographic film, a rival to worldwide brands such as Kodak and Fuji. Then the world started changing—fast.

CEWE saw the change coming better than its rivals did. The digital camera arrived as a mainstream product about 2000. Five years earlier, only 80,000 were sold in Germany. By 2001, that number had exploded to 1.2 million. Today, it's 7.4 million, and the analog film market has all but vanished.

While its rivals pondered what to do about the digital revolution, CEWE acted— investing €350 million in digital photo-finishing capacities even as it restructured its core film business to give it a few more years of life.

Today, CEWE is the leader in online photo and print services. Total revenue is about €528.6 million, providing an EBIT contribution of €29.4 million in 2013. Kodak and Agfa are bankrupt.

The Internet further muddied CEWE's strategic landscape. Its arrival as a consumer phenomenon meant that film and film processing would disappear as businesses when people learned to share digital images online. CEWE responded by teaming with its retailer network to invent and market new photo-finishing products. Soon the company was in the business of photo calendars, posters, canvases, and, in 2006, CEWE PHOTOBOOK.

CEWE didn't invent photobooks. In fact, it was a follower. The company started with established software while also developing its own software for what it knew would become its core business. Eventually, the photobooks spun off a new business: a collection of online printing services grouped under CEWE Print.

Photobooks are now CEWE's flagship product. And yet CEWE is already imagining a day when photobooks shrink in importance. What's next? CEWE thinks the answer will come from mobile devices.

"Our strength is a combination of our foundation for innovation and defining the right innovation strategy," CEO Rolf Hollander says. "It is essential to ensure that employees understand that each technology and product has an end and that the company will have to adapt." If that is to happen, he argues, CEWE will need a culture characterized by open-mindedness and a freedom to dream up the next big thing.

TATA MOTORS GETS SERIOUS ABOUT INNOVATION

In 2000, trouble was on the horizon for Tata Motors. Structural change had come to the Indian auto market, giving pricing power to buyers and posing a threat to the near monopoly Tata enjoyed as the country's largest automaker. Meanwhile, Tata had overdeveloped strengths in segments that were weakening (trucks) and weakness in segments that were growing (small commercial vehicles).

Tata's management was able to spot the trouble just in time, says Tata's former vice chairman Ravi Kant, who retired in 2014. And once it did, Tata moved fast. For example, it expanded its international profile by acquiring Jaguar Land Rover in the United Kingdom and Daewoo Commercial Vehicles in South Korea. But it knew that sustained growth would come not from acquisition but from innovation.

Tata invested heavily in engineering and research attuned to emerging markets, producing passenger cars such as the Safari, India's first sport utility vehicle, and the Nano, marketed as "the world's most affordable car."

The company's most distinctive innovation might be its light truck, the Ace. Since its introduction in 2005, the Ace and its line variants have sold more than a million vehicles. By itself, the Ace created a new category in the Indian automotive market—the small commercial vehicle—which now accounts for more than half of all commercial vehicles sold in India. Tata owns roughly 70 percent of the category it created.

The Ace was the fruit of what Kant calls "structured opportunity identification." What made it commercially viable were innovations to Tata's value chain and, ultimately, to its business model.

The opportunity emerged from an assessment of macroeconomic trends and a firsthand study of customers. Observing the accelerated growth in urban populations likely to characterize the 21st century, for instance, Tata saw strong potential for small vehicles in cities contending with rising congestion. Long term, that may mean the eventual prohibition of heavy commercial vehicles. It also observed a trend that for other manufacturers might have seemed off the radar but which in fact bore directly on the prospect for light commercial vehicles. This was the increasing demand for last-mile goods connectivity driven by the emergence of the hub-and-spoke transportation model.

To test what it was seeing in the data, Tata formed a cross-functional team to interview 4,000 truck and three-wheeler operators in rural and urban markets. The interviews confirmed an appetite for a vehicle with the fuel efficiency, price point, and maneuverability of a three-wheeler but with the safety, durability, and payload capacity of a four-wheeler. The interviews revealed a subtler dimension as well: the aspiration among drivers for the rise in social status that would come from owning a four-wheel truck. From its beginnings, the Ace needed to be all those things.

Development of the Ace was attentive to both speed of innovation and time to profit. To ensure acceptance among cost-sensitive Indian customers, a "target cost approach" was adopted, committing the Ace team to an upper limit on the vehicle's final sticker price. This commitment was a signal of the team's seriousness about pricing innovation. Faster time to profit tightened the team's focus on marketing, distribution, and vendor financing.

"The ability to identify latent demand in the market and not only develop a new product but also manage innovation in a holistic way touched all parts of the value chain," Kant says.

The innovation in Tata's distribution model lay in its expansion of sales outlets close to its target customers in rural and semi-urban areas. Each incumbent dealer was mandated to establish eight to 20 outlets in the targeted region. The company also created "mobile showrooms" and organized displays at village fairs. The objective was multiplying the market's opportunity to, as Kant calls it, "touch and feel" the Ace. Meanwhile, Tata's financing arm supported new customers with long-term loans that made the economics of owning an Ace attractive.

Success was immediate. The production platform was rapidly extended to several variants, including heavier and lighter versions and passenger carriers. Inevitably, Tata has taken many of the innovations associated with the Ace and shared them with its other vehicle lines. Now the fourth-largest truck maker in the world, Tata's revenue in the 2013–2014 fiscal year was a record $38.9 billion.

3M CREATES SPACE FOR ENTREPRENEURSHIP

In 1948, 3M's William McKnight said, "As our business grows, it becomes increasingly necessary to delegate responsibility and to encourage men and women to exercise their initiative. This requires considerable tolerance. Those men and women to whom we delegate authority and responsibility, if they are good people, are going to want to do their jobs in their own way."

McKnight retired in 1966, but 3M has continued demonstrating commitment to individual innovation with what it calls the 15 percent rule. Employees can use 15 percent of their paid time to develop their own ideas. The time is not formally tracked. Instead, it is meant to be a concrete expression of 3M's seriousness about internal innovation.

This culture has paid off for 3M more than once, most famously perhaps in the invention of the Post-it, which started out in 1968 as a failed attempt by chemist Spencer Silver to develop a super-strong glue. 3M's policy of "permitted bootlegging" created room to keep tinkering with this failure. Eventually, another chemist, Art Fry, had the idea of using Silver's tacky glue on the back of a bookmark in a hymnal. It took 10 years, but in 1978, the Post-it was introduced.

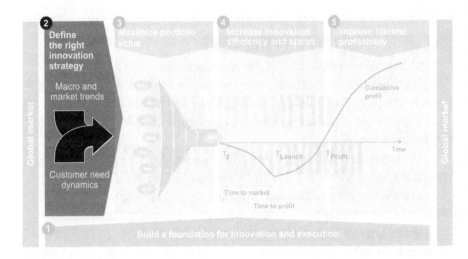

CHAPTER 3

DEFINE THE RIGHT INNOVATION STRATEGY

Tata Motors is India's automotive powerhouse. It is the world's fourth-largest manufacturer of buses and trucks with almost $35 billion in consolidated revenue in 2013. But 10 years ago, Tata realized it had a problem. The world had changed. And Tata didn't notice until it was almost too late.

"Our market had liberalized," remembers Ravi Kant, Tata's former vice chairman. "The world changed from a seller's to a buyer's market, and Tata's monopolistic situation was endangered." The company, he says, realized it was strategically committed to segments that were weakening, such as the very cyclical truck business. Meanwhile, Tata was relatively weak in segments that were growing, such as small commercial vehicles.

Tata responded to this strategic crisis with a new commitment to innovation. Tata's methods and speed reveal a great deal about the right way to define an innovation strategy—not just for a contracting market but for a company's purpose of rejuvenating for the long haul.

In this chapter, we discuss the first steps for forming an innovation strategy, beginning with the population of a search-field portfolio. The search field is the wellhead for a running stream of innovations. As we will see, developing search fields depends on a rigorous point of view about the future—not just of a single company's operating environment but of the world at large, which for good and ill often upends strategic assumptions.

A perspective on the future can't help but determine which segments a company should be thinking about as well as what competencies it will need to own if it is to do more than just think. Competencies need to be geared to where customers are going. That is no easy task when customers can't always say where they think they're headed.

From all these initial steps comes the innovation roadmap, which names the destination and describes how to get there. In this chapter we discuss:

- **Know what you want to achieve.** Have explicit expectations for innovation strategy—its contribution to growth, the segments in which to compete, and what is needed to win. Name the tangible deliverables to which the organization is committed.

- **Own a point of view about the future.** Treat farsightedness as an organizational capability. Structured thinking about the future via strategic *foresighting* introduces a long-term perspective into innovation portfolios and accelerates the speed with which choices are made.

- **Define the innovation search fields.** Prioritize the hunt for commercial ideas at the hunt's earliest stage: the search-field stage. Search fields are the wide end of the innovation funnel, building on trends in the current operating environment and the world at large.

- **Manage to the customer's desired outcome.** Learn what customers want by understanding how customers think about the job they want a product or service to do. The challenge is that customers often don't know what they'll need next.

- **Know your own competencies, and invest accordingly.** Group competencies into two categories: knowledge and talent. The question to answer is which one will be developed internally and which will be bought or borrowed from partners.

- **Draw the innovation roadmap.** Map out the innovation development processes. These are not just about planning and target setting, but also about building in flexibility for the surprises to which even a well-considered view of the future is subject.

KNOW WHAT YOU WANT TO ACHIEVE

Too often in our consulting work, we encounter innovation strategies with vague deliverables (see figure 4). The consequence is an undercooked innovation portfolio. This is not the case with Tata or any of our Best Innovators. Quite the contrary: Best Innovators establish explicit expectations for making the business case for innovation. They name a tangible set of deliverables to which they are committed. Being tangible creates clarity of intent that everyone can see. It

Figure 4
Best Innovators identify clear expectations and deliverables

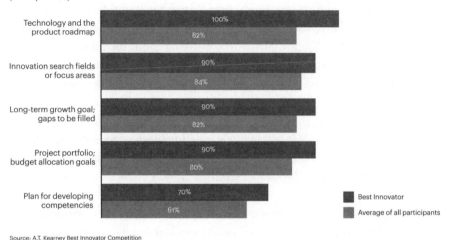

Deliverables
(% responses)

Source: A.T. Kearney Best Innovator Competition

comes from identifying the company's long-term growth goals and saying them out loud for the organization—and investors—to hear.

To build their innovation business case, these leading innovators ask several important questions:

- What is the contribution of innovation to achieving our long-term growth goals, taking into account both the expected development of the current portfolio and the existing innovation pipeline?

- Which market segments will be the focus of the greatest activity?

- What competencies do we need to realize our ambitions for the innovation portfolio? Will they be developed internally or acquired through collaborative partnerships with suppliers, say, or universities?

- What is the right mix for the innovation portfolio in terms of low- versus high-risk and short- versus long-term projects? What is the right mix in terms of new markets and new technologies versus incremental improvement in processes and products (or frugal innovation, as it is sometimes called)?[5] Which should be given prioritized acceleration in the innovation pipeline?

- What is the required innovation speed? In other words, how fast do we need to get there, and what is the roadmap for getting us there?

- How will innovation strategy be woven into the daily work of a globally distributed business—among employees, certainly, but among stakeholders and partners as well?

These questions are not meant as a narrowing down of the innovation horizon. Quite the opposite: they widen the horizon. Working through the questions produces a view into the subjects that the organization needs to focus on to begin building its future.

A well-balanced innovation portfolio integrates mid-range and long-term components. It includes projects in beta and projects on their way to being launched.

OWN A POINT OF VIEW ABOUT THE FUTURE

"A product that is market ready," observes QIAGEN CEO Peer Schatz, "is always the result of cooperation among different departments—from R&D and strategy to production and sales." This kind of cross-functional conversation is essential to the foresight that great innovators manifest in their innovation strategies. This is particularly true in the early stage of an innovation strategy, when an organization is still defining its search fields.

Characteristic of Best Innovators is an articulate view of the future, one that can be described in both macro and micro terms. Formally thinking about where the world is going introduces a long-term perspective into their innovation portfolios. And by long term, we mean years out into the future. For Best Innovators, that sort of view is essential to knowing where to bet their money. They want to shape the world before it shapes them.

Thinking rigorously about the future is hard. There are lots of ways to try it. In a given industry, discernment and foresight take many shapes specific to a given business. If the Best Innovators' varied processes for thinking about tomorrow have one thing in common, it is that all of them treat farsightedness as a central pillar of their innovation strategies—particularly as change in the world alters the evolution of what customers want.

Probably the most well-known methodology for thinking about the future is scenario analysis, although it's not always the most understood. Whatever the approach, the language of scenario planning pervades the conversation of companies at work on discerning the future. For example, they speak of drivers—the large forces shaping not just the immediate operating environment but our world in general. Since the future never arrives in quite the way we expect, managers working on innovation portfolios with long tails test multiple strategic and tactical scenarios to judge whether their plans will thrive in unexpected conditions.

Especially since the credit crisis of 2008, managers with a professional interest in the future speak in terms of being resilient in the face of wildcards, or "Black Swans."[6] These are low-probability, high-impact events that directly affect the human condition—and company operating environments—that no one sees coming but which in hindsight can appear to have been inevitable.

Whatever the method for thinking about the future, the goal is to avoid blind spots. No business wants to be taken unaware by threats. Even more painful is missing opportunities created by transformational moments.

An informed point of view about the future is implicit in developing an innovation strategy and defining search fields. Innovation managers begin by thinking as broadly as possible about where the drivers in their immediate operating environment and the world at large are headed. What themes can be derived from the changes these drivers are likely to provoke? What do the themes have in common? How would we group these commonalities into super themes? The objective is to free strategists of any tendency to look at the future as pretty much like the recent past, only different.

"People always look at the future as an extrapolation of the past," says Guy Wollaert, Coca-Cola's chief technology officer. "It is as if they don't believe in growth. If you don't extrapolate from the past, you are better prepared to be on the offensive and capture opportunities, whether they stem from a technological development or shifting consumer needs."

For Best Innovators, discerning these opportunities is not the one-off product of a corporate retreat. A shared perspective on the future is instead the conversation starter in a continual strategic dialogue. Foresight is a capability, an ongoing part of operational management that assures the strength of a long-term strategic view. It is an active influence on their strategic choices. It accelerates the speed with which choices can be made. It is comprehensive in scope, shaping and aligning the outlook—and the innovation portfolio—of the entire organization, no matter what size.

This sort of multilevel conversation should not take place solely inside a headquarters building. It needs to include voices from across the company and from outside, including customers (*especially* customers), suppliers, universities, consultants, and other collaborators no matter where they sit.

Thinking about the future in detail is an existential necessity for Best Innovators, especially those with a worldwide profile.

"Markets and segments are changing everywhere in the world," explains Volkswagen CTO Ulrich Hackenberg. "Customer requirements are becoming more and more challenging, and the demand for sustainable vehicle and drive concepts is growing. In the future, cars will need to offer more functionality to accommodate more individualized customer needs."

A global entity such as Volkswagen is obliged to think in detail about the future of markets and cultures to which it is not native. For example, Volkswagen is running a significant venture in China called the People's Car Project. Its sole purpose is to get closer to what its mainly young Chinese customers are thinking about Volkswagen's car line and where that may lead the company in the future.

For the persistently innovative (and those that want to be), the task is to tune in to where customers are going, usually before they even know where they're headed.

DEFINE THE INNOVATION SEARCH FIELDS

The early work on innovation strategy should be all about creating transparency, starting with a clear view of the trends inside and outside of the current operating environment. A rigorous innovation business case will prioritize the hunt for new commercial ideas at the earliest point: the search-field stage.

The Best Innovators are conspicuous not just for building innovation portfolios but for the varieties of ways in which they go about it. Whatever the approach, every search-field portfolio begins with a question: in which market segments, indeed in which industries, do we plan to compete not just today but in the future?

Depending on the industry and the competitive situation, Best Innovators have different ways of framing this question. Tata Motors, for example, developed its search fields with the intent of raising its profile in India's small-car segment. For its search-field portfolio, it developed a hypothesis that growth would be driven by several factors with which the organization needed to become better acquainted. One factor was rising income among Indians, which was improving the quality of life for middle-class drivers and prompting their desire to increase their social status. Tata's theory was that this would also prompt a shift in demand from three-wheeled vehicles to four-wheeled. Much needed to be done before products could be developed, but Tata's broadly defined search field is where these products would begin. The process was uncommonly rapid. In 2008, Tata launched the Nano as the world's cheapest passenger car at just $2,000.

Germany's Volkswagen, which won the 2005 Best Innovator award in the sustainable innovation category, fills the wide end of its innovation funnel with a classically broad set of search fields, including categories such as environmental protection laws, regulation, new competition, and region-specific prod-ucts. The last is of special importance—and a special challenge—to a company that oper-ates 104 factories around the globe with more than 550,000 employees building roughly 280 models.

> *"Innovation is not an island. It has its sources across the whole company, and the drive toward innovation can't be dogmatically pressed into systems. Many different influences affect innovation success, from serendipity to structured processes."*
>
> Peer Schatz
> CEO
> QIAGEN

"Innovation for us isn't just the icing on the cake," says chief technology officer Ulrich Hackenberg. "It's an integral part of our development activities."

It is also an essential part of the Volkswagen brand strategy. For a company with the motto "Das Auto," the expansiveness manifest in its search fields is fundamental to its identity—and to navigating an industry that is in a state of perpetual volatility. The company communicates this plainly to both the orga-nization and its shareholders.

"The automotive industry is experiencing radical transformations," chair-man Martin Winterkorn wrote in the company's 2012 annual report. "Markets and segments are changing, customer requirements are becoming more and more challenging, and the demand for sustainable vehicle and drive concepts is growing. Future cars will need to offer more functionality to comply with more diverse and individual customer needs."

In Volkswagen's traditional markets around the world, new players are appearing, and industry volumes are decreasing. Meanwhile, the company is working to make sense of issues such as climate change, scarce resources, the aging of societies, and the inexorable growth of cities. It expects all of them to have big impacts on the car industry.

By 2050, for example, the world's population is expected to grow to nine billion people. Up to 70 percent of them will live in cities. Volkswagen sees a direct strategic connection to the choices it will need to make. Population growth and urban density will heighten the importance of alternative powertrains, for instance, as well as the need for intelligent traffic management. Volkswagen envisions a place for itself in both these businesses and includes them among its search fields as part of its innovation strategy.

Search fields build on macro trends such as alterations in consumption patterns, demographics, technology, political movements, and even the natural environment. Take Kapsch, for example, the Austrian maker of telecommunication systems and traffic-monitoring technologies for which the urbanization of our planet and the dream of smart cities is a growing preoccupation. Then there is Rosenbauer, a world leader in firefighting equipment, which has taken note of the phenomenal mobility of people in the countries where it operates, limiting the population available for fire service. What might that mean for Rosenbauer? For one thing, it could mean more women will become firefighters, a demographic not included until very recently. Rosenbauer is asking what that might mean for its equipment line.

Big trends are the starting point of a search-field portfolio, the seeds that may one day germinate. However, it is too soon to be thinking in detail about how a macro trend will eventually give birth to a specific product.

Search fields are a guide to making choices. They focus idea generation in areas that have either high business potential or strategic importance. And there must be a direct link to current business strategy. For example, 3M produces a Markets of the Future analysis annually.

In the early stages of an innovation strategy, a company need not be first class in every segment in its search-field portfolio. Search fields start a company down the path toward determining the areas where it wants to become first class. They point the way toward the competencies the business will need to acquire—one way or another—to fully realize its innovation strategy's potential in support of new growth.

This is the deliverable of an innovation strategy. An organization owes this to itself, and there can be nothing vague about it.

There is no single best practice for developing search fields. Most of the Best Innovators have evolved idiosyncratic methods that suit the characteristics of their companies. But no matter which way Best Innovators go about defining and filling their search-field portfolios, all of them include a point of view about the future—a perspective that is both expansive and rigorous.

MANAGE TO THE CUSTOMER'S DESIRED OUTCOME

Every company, Best Innovator or not, wants to know what its customers think. "Left to ourselves to come up with ways to provide value, our solutions would be confined to better performance and fuel efficiency, or something to that effect," says Komatsu CEO Tetsuji Ohashi. "The result would be limited in terms of what construction equipment can become. Simply improving a product's functionality gives you the industrial position of a follower."

> *"Innovation isn't the icing on the cake. It's an integral part of our development activities."*
>
> Ulrich Hackenberg
> CTO
> Volkswagen

Learning *what* customers think depends on an understanding of *how* they think. It's all in how you ask.

We are still surprised to see how often even very successful companies pursue innovation strategies with not much more than a good hunch about what customers want. In some cases, this is because of a weak organizational culture that underemphasizes closeness to the customer—a culture, as Ohashi puts it, that fails to take "achieving the dreams of its customers" as its starting point. (See the preceding chapter, "Build the Foundation for Innovation and Execution.")

Even among companies with an active attachment to customers, we see inefficiencies in the work of extracting intelligence from what they are hearing.

If you want customers to explain what they need, don't ask them directly. Instead, ask why they buy a product or a service—in other words, the *job* they want it to do. Then listen closely to the response. Describing the use to which they want to put a product pinpoints unmet needs and niches awaiting innovation. We call this the *desired outcome* approach to customer intelligence. (See sidebar: "A Clean Measure of Customer Need" on page 62.)

Traditional methods of listening to customers include a variety of valuable qualitative and quantitative tools. Ethnographic observation, for instance, is associated with design thinking. It entails watching customers use a product or service in their "natural habitat," which yields direct insight into the customer experience. In-depth interviews with individual customers using open-ended questions offer the flexibility to probe unanticipated issues. Focus groups provide a different sort of insight that comes from watching customers bounce off one another's ideas. Quantitative surveys lack this human dynamic but do produce statistically significant analysis and allow for quantitatively rigorous segmentation of needs.

However, the difficulty in these traditional methods is that customers often don't know what they need next, or they can't describe it. Their answer to a direct question—"What do you want?"—is likely to be a mash-up of abstract needs, problems, wished-for benefits, specifications, solutions, distractions, latent needs, must-haves, and so on into a confusing mix that leaves its meaning up to the intuition of the questioner.

A good example of how challenging it can be to really know what customers want comes from Henkel Laundry & Home Care. For years, the business unit heard customers express their desire for environmentally sound products. But at the same time, customers were unwilling to pay more for these products. Henkel's solution to this apparent contradiction was to link green products to the savings generated from lower energy costs.

Perhaps just as often, companies don't really know what information they want from customers—a situation made no less difficult by the variety of ways in which "customer need" is interpreted by different departments within a company.

The desired outcome approach builds on a combination of traditional methods but gives them new precision, starting with creating a shared understanding of "need" inside the organization. It enables an explicit description of customer values, even when those values are latent. This makes it easier to translate customer language into engineer's language. And *that* gives tight focus to the innovation strategy—as well as greater speed—by directing innovation efforts toward a defined set of opportunities.

For many Best Innovators, the desired outcome approach seems to come naturally. As Komatsu's Ohashi puts it, "Continued innovation from understanding customers and working with them to achieve their dreams creates a business format—a business model, say, or new technologies—that will not be copied overnight."

Ohashi would recognize kindred spirits at LINET, the path-breaking European manufacturer of hospital and nursing beds that won the Best Innovator award the first year it was held in the Czech Republic in 2012.

"We don't expect customers to come to us with improvement suggestions on their own initiative," says LINET executive director Tomáš Kolář. "We actively cooperate with staff. We organize moderated discussions to explore how medical staff work and anticipate what might make their work easier and so improve the patient's comfort."

LINET is especially attuned to customer complaints, which it reads as requests for specific kinds of product changes and evaluates for innovation potential. LINET's well-received smart beds, which monitor a patient's vital signs, were developed in exactly this way. Kolář estimates that this customer input is responsible for 50 percent of LINET's innovation portfolio—double the contribution of patent searches and in-house brainstorming.

KNOW YOUR OWN COMPETENCIES, AND INVEST ACCORDINGLY

Competencies can be broadly grouped into two categories: knowledge and talent. These amount to the same thing. The question a Best Innovator has to answer is which competencies will be required to support its innovation strategy. Will they be developed internally, or will they be bought?

For Best Innovators, the assembly of competencies is a puzzle put together with a view less to the present than to the future. The final piece is owning the right mix of talent.

"When it comes to pursuing innovation," Ohashi says, "simply being smart or being familiar with technology is not enough." Komatsu takes its interest in the customer experience to such an extent that it sometimes hires employees of the customer. Sometimes, it even acquires the customer. For example, the company has hired people who worked in mines in the United States, people with in-depth knowledge not just of individual pieces of machinery but of how the machinery is used. As a result, Komatsu is doing more than getting closer to its customers. It is deliberately acquiring the competencies dictated by its innovation strategy.

At other times, Komatsu has taken the acquisition route to, in Ohashi's words, "internalize external knowledge." In 1996, for example, it bought Modular Mining Systems, Inc., to get a better grasp of the needs of customers who manage mining operations. The acquisition paid off handsomely when combined with the company's existing knowledge base.

Volkswagen, to consider another example, takes special interest in building a culture of continuous learning, including what it calls

> "When it comes to pursuing innovation, simply being smart or being familiar with technology is not enough."
>
> Tetsuji Ohashi
> President and CEO
> Komatsu

"demand-oriented and tailored qualification" alongside its development of new training formats for personnel.

ČKD Group may not be a colossus like Komatsu or Volkswagen, yet within its power and energy segments, the Czech engineering firm is a force. "We're not a major player in terms of size," says CEO Jan Musil. "We don't have the long-lasting relationships like our larger competitors, and that definitely puts us at a disadvantage. We need to apply high-quality competitive pressure."

However, ČKD uses its smaller size as an advantage. One such advantage is nimbleness in its attention to movements in its market segments. So is alertness to gaps in its ability to respond.

"It's important for us to know exactly what technical elements new systems contain," Musil says, "and who's currently the global leader for supplying these systems." ČKD buys or develops whatever knowledge it does not own. Suppliers, for example, habitually become partners, integrated into the company to achieve what Musil calls "complementary competence" that helps both parties win future tenders.

Inside or outside the organization, ČKD emphasizes the closeness of its collaborations to amplify competencies—another advantage of its smaller size.

"We work on the principle of a low power distance," says Musil, borrowing an idea developed by the Dutch social psychologist and former IBM engineer Geert Hofstede to measure the distribution of power in organizations and society generally.[7] "The members of our teams know each other," Musil says, "and relationships became personal. There needs to be a fit on a personal level—to be of the same blood type, if you will. We build bonds of friendship, which makes us more capable of pushing on the organizational level than if we did not have these bonds."

Fostering innovation starts with recruiting the right talent, says Gildeon Filho, Chemtech's director of operations. When an organization is thinking 10 or even 15 years out, it must perpetually replenish its talent pipeline and constantly review the match of talent and other competencies it needs to maximize the value of its innovation portfolio.

And it must do one more thing: draw the roadmap to get where it wants to go.

DRAW THE INNOVATION ROADMAP

Best Innovators are future-oriented, by habit and by intention. Their innovation strategies are built with planning tools for both the short term (one to three years) and the long term. All draw some variant of what we call innovation road-maps—detailing the steps of the development process from design all the way through production and product launch. Their mapmakers make connections between innovation happening in one product area and possible applications elsewhere in the product portfolio.[8]

Roadmaps are not just about planning and target setting. They build in flexibility for the inevitable surprises to which even a well-considered view of the future is subject. The roadmap is a refined deliverable of an innovation strategy.

For the Best Innovators, the roadmap is about more than just budget and staffing. An innovation roadmap describes when a new technology or product will be brought to market, and it names the inventory of competencies that will be required to make this happen. The roadmap tells the organization not only which product or services will be brought to market but also how fast and in what format, with clear guidance for budget allocation.

In a certain sense, developing a roadmap is a problem that solves itself: if I know when I need to have my product ready, I am compelled to ask the necessary questions about what I'll need to hit my deliverable.

Valeo CEO Jacques Aschenbroich credits what he calls "structured and frequent exchanges with customers" with a lead role in creating the French company's innovation roadmap. "An exchange of views with our customers on our respective technological roadmaps," he says, "enables Valeo to drive priority topics and anticipate solutions expected by our customers and their own end-user clients."

Valeo is an independent automotive supplier partner to all automakers worldwide. As a technology company, Valeo proposes products and systems that contribute to the reduction of CO_2 emissions by automobiles and to the development of intuitive driving. The company won a Best Innovator award in 2007 in the innovation-processes category. Valeo has also been ranked in Thomson Reuters' Top 100 Global Innovators since 2012.

"We review technology roadmaps twice a year," Aschenbroich says, "and carefully check the state of our innovation portfolio versus societal needs such as emission reduction or intuitive driving, customer demand, and market orientations."

In our work with Best Innovators, we've seen roadmaps that take three or even 10 years to reach peak impact. Along the way, there are commercial milestones, naturally. But if nothing else, a roadmap that looks out that far is a tonic for organizations that might otherwise drift into the rut of short-term planning—the rut that can sideline an innovation portfolio.

Best Innovators have a notable clarity of strategic direction. They know what they want and are specific in what they expect their innovation effort to deliver—in terms of profitability and in every other regard.

Strategic clarity defines innovation's long-term meaning for profitable growth. It generates search fields, to begin with, and the competencies needed to support an ambitious innovation portfolio. It identifies the segments in which a business will compete. It widens horizons.

Clarity, so galvanizing to organizations and to partners, is vital in the early work of innovation strategy. Before anything else, it should be about creating transparency. Transparency originates in a structured view into trends inside and outside of a Best Innovator's current operating environment. This structured view shapes the creation of search fields.

The foresight so intrinsic to the population of search fields builds on macro trends inside and outside of the current operating environment. Explicit in the creation of search fields is active reflection about where the world is taking the business. Thinking about the direction in which the wider world is headed imbues search fields and the whole innovation strategy with a long-term perspective that, for Best Innovators, is typically years out into the future.

The other major force shaping the creation of an innovation portfolio is the customer, or more specifically the customer's desired outcomes. Best Innovators listen to customers with an intensity that yields understanding of where their needs are headed—often before customers themselves know.

This attention to the future and to customers provides not resiliency but continuous refreshment of strategy. In that respect, innovation roadmaps provide a complementary constancy, describing the path to profitable growth and what the business will need if it is to get where it wants to go. From design through production to product launch, Best Innovators are thinking not only about budgets and staff but also about the crucial elements of idea development—format, skills, knowledge, innovation speed—which among their peers are too often discussed in an under-structured, under-thought way. For Best Innovators, these elements are crucial to optimizing the value of an innovation portfolio.

THE LANGUAGE OF SCENARIO PLANNING

Drivers: the central economic and social forces shaping the global environment
Change themes: individual developments within each global driver
Super themes: individual themes condensed to a larger group based on convergence
New trends: groupings of themes across drivers based on association—or conflict—with one another
Scenario: a potential positive or negative development of a trend derived from change themes or wildcards
Wildcard discontinuity: a low-probability, extremely high-impact event that directly affects the human condition; may be either positively or negatively disruptive; fast-moving and beyond the control of any institution, group, or individual; sometimes called a "Black Swan" event

THE USES OF SCENARIO PLANNING

Everyone has a picture of the future in his or her head. Problems arise when this view is unstated but still acted upon. Scenario planning makes this worldview explicit by helping planners think out loud about more than one possible future.

The ancestry of modern scenario-planning methods is usually traced to Royal Dutch Shell in the 1970s.[9] Like others in its industry, Shell was caught off guard by the seemingly sudden political assertiveness of OPEC nations and by the emergence of the environmental movement—phenomena that were well outside the company's expertise in drilling and refining 40 years ago. Shell needed a new way of imagining its operating environment. It needed to understand the meaning of external forces for the tactical choices it would have to make if the company was to grow.

There are many kinds of scenario planning, all of which have their followers. Each approach focuses on the search for transformational moments—radical developments that can alter the way we work or even the way we live. These are high-impact, border-crossing, and often without alternatives. It is not uncommon for such drivers to hit peak impact only after 10 or 15 years.

The point to keep in mind is that scenario planning should never be about developing all possible futures and then betting on the most likely. It is about harvesting all the insights derived from applying a hypothetical strategy to a range of plausible futures and then observing which behaviors are optimal for the organization and its innovation strategy. That way, an organization's chosen path, and the capabilities it builds to pursue that path, will serve it no matter what kind of future arrives.[10]

Skeptics often contend that, in practice, scenario planning is a stimulating intellectual exercise disconnected from day-to-day choices. If the work is managed poorly, this is true. Managing it correctly begins with picking the right mix of participants—outsiders with informed perspectives on the world at large and expert insiders who act on the insights derived from the work.

Formal scenario analysis tends to work best for large, multidimensional organizations. For insiders, participating in scenario planning creates alignment built on a shared vocabulary for talking about the future. If an innovation manager says, "I think we're moving into such-and-such world," the tag immediately triggers a specific response among colleagues who understand the reference to a universe they've explored together. This is not groupthink. It is shared participation in a spectrum of possibilities that managers all understand and can talk about, even when they disagree on its implications. Contention becomes easier to deal with, even useful to have. This is strategic foresight at its most concrete.

There may be as many approaches to scenario planning as there are practitioners, but certain best practices are worth remembering. The first is senior sponsorship, which signals not only the organization's seriousness but also assures the authority to act quickly on portfolio opportunities (and if need be on risk mitigation). A good guarantee of completeness—and authority to take action—is to make scenario planning a function with visible corporate sponsorship.

Done right, scenario planning produces an integrated and resilient set of insights into the mid- and long-term future. The thing about the future, though, is that it's always in motion. Best practice, therefore, is an annual review of where the long view may be taking us.

A CLEAN MEASURE OF CUSTOMER NEED

The desired outcome-based voice-of-the-customer methodology uses a framework of customer "jobs to be done" and the "desired outcomes" for these jobs, as proposed by Clayton Christensen and Anthony Ulwick.[11,12] The method is based on the assumption that customers "hire" a product or service to help them accomplish a specific job, for example to safely carry them and their belongings from point A to point B or to keep their faces smooth and free of facial hair.

Associated with each job is a desired outcome—the customer's ideal for a job well done. It is a way to define and measure how well the product performs to accomplish the targeted job. A desired outcome might be to minimize the jerking motion of a passenger and his belongings while riding on a bus or to minimize the time it takes to complete a bank transaction.

In this framework, jobs-to-be-done and desired-outcome statements use specific and consistent grammatical structure. This allows them to be unambiguously understood, easily compared, and readily translated into technical specifications while maintaining layperson's language.

The desired-outcome statements are the customer needs. With this systematic and consistent language as a basic framework, we can gather information about what customers want using words they understand. Then, we can easily compare them and translate them into technical targets.

COELCE TAKES OPERATIONAL PATH TO INNOVATION

Almost nine million people in the Brazilian state of Ceará depend on Coelce for their electricity. Coelce—a subsidiary of Enel, through Enersis, a multinational group based in Italy and a leading integrated player in the power and gas markets of Europe and Latin America—is the sole distributor in Ceará under a concession granted by the Brazilian government through 2028. The utility employs 6,558 people and operates more than 136,000 kilometers of energy distribution lines.

About 13 years ago, Coelce began a long-term strategic planning effort that focused on expansion built on service improvement. Getting closer to clients was the centerpiece of the effort, a determination signaled in the company's new motto: "Our idea is to know you."

Inside Coelce, the idea of an aggressive innovation effort by a utility with a regulated competitive scope was at first resisted. By 2012, 10 years after the push began, the company's culture had been transformed.

For an electricity distributor, innovation can be leveraged in two ways, explains CEO Abel Rochinha. The first is technology development, which corresponds to advances in the distributor's infrastructure. This is expensive and can be easily copied. The second way is the operational path, including improvements and efficiency gains on daily processes. It is less capital intensive than new-technology development and has to be developed entirely within the company. For Coelce, the operational approach was the lever of its strategic innovation, the differentiator between Coelce and other Brazilian utilities.

By 2012, Coelce's investment in creating an innovation culture was paying off. That was the year the company was elected best distributor of electricity in Brazil and won the Abradee Award, given annually by the Brazilian Association of Electricity Distributors. It was also the year Brazil's National Agency of Electrical Energy gave Coelce first place in its national ranking. And it was the year Coelce received the Best Innovator award.

SEEDS OF TECHNOLOGICAL INNOVATION LEAD TO GROWTH FOR KOMATSU

In 2009 at the bottom of the global financial crisis, Komatsu was named to A.T. Kearney's Global Champions list. For this construction and mining equipment maker, the second-largest in the world after Caterpillar, the strength of its business during a worldwide recession seemed to defy gravity.

Whereas Caterpillar achieved success by expanding and intensifying its regional coverage, chiefly by strengthening ties with dealers, Komatsu's strategy has been to capitalize on technological innovation in its products and services.

Komatsu would be on any list of companies with a commitment to innovation that is undeterred by near-term economic bumps. "It's important to establish the means to grow without crushing the seeds of innovation if they're not immediately exposed to the sun," says CEO Tetsuji Ohashi.

A good example is the unmanned dump truck, the Autonomous Haulage System. Introduction of that product had to wait until global positioning satellites were opened for private use. While Komatsu waited, it worked on the sensor and communications technologies that constitute the truck's onboard IT system.

Innovation tends to create the condition for successor innovations. Komatsu's proprietary GPS system, KOMTRAX, was introduced in 2001 largely as a theft-protection technology. What soon became clear was that KOMTRAX could also communicate information about how hard and how much a piece of equipment was working. That allowed Komatsu to capture information about more than just maintenance schedules, and it indirectly served to signal market conditions, which Komatsu uses to adjust production schedules.

"Making a dump truck run without the need for an operator is a simple technological innovation," says Ohashi. "But combining an operational control system with the technology to perform autonomous operation has helped achieve an optimal level of operational control for all mining processes, including those involving manned vehicles," he says. "That changed the way our customers work. That's true innovation."

NEW TALENT AND KNOWLEDGE "REOXYGENATE" IDEAS AT CHEMTECH

Chemtech was founded in Brazil in 1989. By the time it was acquired by Siemens in 2001, it was already building a worldwide profile as a provider of engineering IT and consulting to process industries such as oil and gas, petrochemicals, and power generation.

In a market that is becoming more commoditized, with a growing pressure to lower prices, director of operations Gildeon Filho believes the company's passion for developing innovative solutions that generate value for its clients makes Chemtech stand apart from its competitors.

With unremitting pressure to grow what it knows, regular infusions of new knowledge are an operational necessity. Since 2010, for instance, Chemtech has made open innovation a centerpiece of its operational process with exactly that goal in mind. Pivotal to this effort are Chemtech partnerships with other R&D centers in Brazil and around the world.[13] The nurturing—and protection—of intellectual property is a central element of Chemtech's open-innovation approach, as it must be for any innovator.

Chemtech is also distinctive in its preoccupation with infusions of new talent, a preoccupation specifically cited in its Best Innovator award in 2011. Its New Talents program, for example, recruits the best students from top universities and technical programs for a yearlong training program—all expenses paid. In just the first three years, New Talents recruited and trained more than 1,500 technicians and engineers from across Brazil.

The effect of bringing in the best new talent and mixing them with experienced professionals, Filho says, is a "reoxygenation of ideas."

The impact of New Talents on Chemtech's innovation culture is evident in demographic terms. Roughly 85 percent of Chemtech employees are younger than 35, as are about 60 percent of senior leadership.

Participants in the program are expected to be contributors right from the start. Chemtech Research & Development, for instance, launched a tool for assertively managing its innovation portfolio called Chem Inova, which the company traces directly to an idea contributed by New Talents. Chem Inova centralizes the management of new product ideas and assures strategic alignment. This includes developing business plans and assessing the prospective impact for customers.

When it was introduced in 2013, Chem Inova rapidly roughed out 50 new ideas. Out of these, seven were quickly scheduled for implementation.

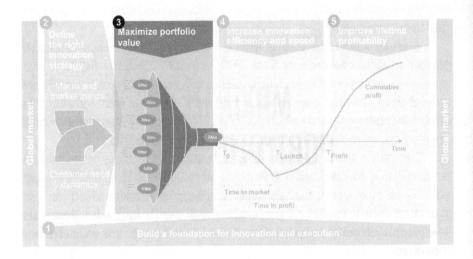

CHAPTER 4
MAXIMIZE
PORTFOLIO VALUE

For components suppliers in the automotive industry, the pressure to remain relevant is relentless and accelerating. The breadth of what they are expected to do is enormous. For example, they must improve the efficiency of conventional combustion engines on one hand, and collaborate with carmakers to advance electric cars on the other. Somewhere in between those two expectations is accommodating millions of drivers who have come to think of their automobiles as a branch of consumer electronics, including functioning as cradles for their mobile devices.[14]

For the Valeo Group, the French automotive supplier that won a 2007 Best Innovator award, the special challenge lies in managing an innovation strategy for four business units employing 9,000 research people across 16 research centers and 34 development centers in 19 countries.

"The industry no longer stands at a single place," says CEO Jacques Aschenbroich, an engineer who ran the high-performance materials effort at Saint-Gobain S.A. before joining Valeo in 2008. "Our R&D employees are spread all across the world to be close to our customers, and they work on a multitude of product and process technologies. If we are continuously challenging our existing products, we need an innovation process that maintains the balance between rigor and flexibility."

Rigor and flexibility are in a sense the controlling terms of this book. Ours is an anti-romantic account of developing innovation strategy and optimizing the value of the innovation portfolio. This chapter is the hinge of our account, describing how companies such as Valeo and other winners of the Best Innovator award institutionalize innovation in a repeatable way and amplify their investment for the long haul.

This chapter is about optimizing the value in an innovation portfolio. It describes best practices—from the portfolio's earliest stages (the search fields)

> *"If we are continuously challenging our existing products, we need an innovation process that maintains the balance between rigor and flexibility."*
>
> Jacques Aschenbroich
> CEO
> Valeo

to prioritizing ideas and selecting the ones to develop and launch as money-making innovations, all the way through their eventual supplanting by new innovations. This is the innovation life cycle.

At almost every stage in an idea's development, collaborations at every level of an organization make the concept richer and more protean. Nourishing and recognizing employees' commercial creativity is a central pillar of a culture of innovation, as we saw in the chapter "Build the Foundation for Innovation and Execution." But collaboration also embraces the wide range of external players from customers and suppliers to universities, government agencies, and, in special cases, even competitors. More and more, it includes innovation "brokers" acting as matchmakers between partners that see in one another capabilities that their own organizations lack.

IN PRAISE OF INCREMENTAL INNOVATION

The cliché of our era is disruptive innovation—the big idea that changes everything. But not every idea in an innovation portfolio needs to be a disruption. Incremental innovation has its place in the mix as well.

Consider, for example, Companhia Energetica do Ceará (Coelce), the privately held Brazilian power company that won a Best Innovator award in 2012 and 2013. Coelce operates under a concession granted by the Brazilian government in Ceará, a largely undeveloped region of the country. Given these circumstances, the very idea of innovation seemed nearly pointless inside Coelce for a long time. But 11 years ago, with an eye to the future development of the Ceará region, the company embarked on a program of incremental innovation that reduced operating costs, lowered accident rates, and improved quality. In five years (2008 to 2013), it developed a portfolio of 304 innovation possibilities. The value of these largely incremental innovations to the company, so far, is estimated at about $10.43 million.

In innovation studies, a great deal has been written about disruption, as if social and technological upheaval is the only worthwhile objective of an innovation strategy. This is wrong. If a company bets only on blockbusters, it will have no growth trajectory. In fact, it will be fortunate to have a stable future of any kind. An innovation portfolio must balance both disruption and incremental innovation. Disruptions are transformative moments in the life of an organization. They not only can produce a sudden acceleration in the top line but also move a company into an entirely new industry sector. However, year over year profitability depends on incremental innovation. The IMP³rove benchmarking database shows that the focus on radical and incremental innovation might also correlate with the size of the organization. In the group of small companies with 20 employees or fewer, 20 percent say they are striving for radical innovation, while in the group of small companies with 100 or more employees, only 14 percent aim for radical innovation. The share of companies that innovate to change the competitive environment with incremental innovation is between 42 percent for the small companies with fewer than 20 employees and 49 percent for companies with 100 or more employees.[15]

Either way, an organization is ahead of the curve when it manages the total value of its innovation portfolio for optimal return. In this chapter, we discuss:

- **Manage your innovation portfolio.** Conceive a new business pipeline not as one portfolio but as five in sequence, each a stage gate on the road from market insight to product launch, each governed by performance metrics that define the innovation life cycle.

- **Pursue truly open innovation.** Leverage the capabilities of external players to optimize their own innovation performance; embrace a wide range of external players, including customers, suppliers, universities, government agencies, and in special cases, competitors.

- **Boost the idea transfer rate.** At every stage gate, a concept must justify its right to exist. Transfer rate describes how many concepts survive this journey through the innovation funnel. A low rate means wasted time—and money—on too many duds. A high rate means efficiency in funnel management.

MANAGE YOUR INNOVATION PORTFOLIO

The process of taking a concept from insight to product launch is often described using the metaphor of a funnel. In the early stage, the funnel is very wide. This makes sense: lots of ideas are fermenting, and everything is open for discussion. But the funnel becomes disproportionately narrow at its end. Something dramatic happens in between.

The narrow point is the active management of the innovation portfolio as potential innovations move from search fields to product launch. This involves a winnowing of ideas, of course. But beyond the winnowing, it requires balancing a company's full portfolio of business initiatives, which is the same as balancing the innovation strategy.

NAMING THE PARTS OF THE PIPELINE

The real-world experience of Best Innovators leads us to view the new business pipeline not as one portfolio but as five, each a stage on the path to product or service launch (see figure 5). The stage-gate approach should not be applied as a harness, but should leave appropriate room for flexibility. What is remarkable is how each Best Innovator develops a homegrown approach to managing the innovation life cycle in a way that fits the metaphor of the narrowing funnel,

Figure 5

Best Innovators manage the life cycle of the innovation portfolio

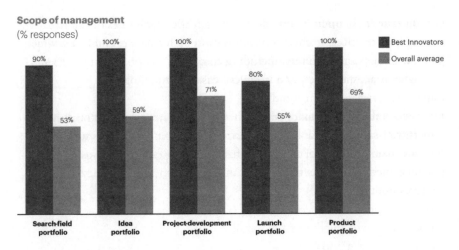

Scope of management
(% responses)

Best Innovators
Overall average

Search-field portfolio — 90% / 53%
Idea portfolio — 100% / 59%
Project-development portfolio — 100% / 71%
Launch portfolio — 80% / 55%
Product portfolio — 100% / 69%

Source: A.T. Kearney Best Innovator Competition

taking new business ideas from their broadest beginnings to more refined products or services ready for the world.

Best Innovators excel in creating transparent processes that allow them to see the progress of their innovation strategy from a market insight to a product launch. In the chapter "Define the Right Innovation Strategy," we discussed the foundational portfolio of the new business pipeline: search fields. Search fields build on macro trends at work in the world within a specific operating environment and beyond. They are a hunting ground for unaddressed trends, threats, and opportunities. This is the part of the innovation portfolio where seeds are sown. It may be the wide end of the funnel, but even at this early stage, it filters new concepts through an expectation of alignment with the organization's strategic goals (even though it may take the organization and its goals to unexpected places).

Consider Société Nationale des Chemins de fer Français (SNCF), the French national railway that won a 2013 Best Innovator award in the services category for its Voyages unit. SNCF is Europe's leading provider of high-speed and long-distance rail. The pressure on SNCF to innovate is accelerating with the liberalization of European rail service, which began with the opening of a freight service in 2007 and a passenger service in 2010.[16] Barbara Dalibard, who has headed the Voyages division since 2010, says SNCF defined a search field built on its customers' broadly defined desire for mobility. What the company meant by that was not mere transportation from one station to another. That, after all, is the minimal expectation of a railway, its core business.

What customers were looking for was service to and from the starting and ending points of their journeys. As Dalibard told *EURAILmag*, "Our TGV services portfolio aims to simplify the lives of customers from steps A to Z in their journey—starting from purchasing and printing e-tickets at home, taking children during the journey, and luggage handling for older customers."[17]

The goal, she says, "is a seamless customer experience from end to end."[18] From this broad understanding of what customers were saying, SNCF built an *idea portfolio*. This broad collection of concepts—still pure potential energy—extracts the most promising concepts from search fields. For SNCF, it led to experimentation with unconventional services for passengers who might otherwise choose different modes of transportation or who might not travel at all.

> "The dilemma is how to establish some form of organizational ambidexterity."
>
> Georg Kapsch
> CEO
> Kapsch TrafficCom

Creating an idea portfolio is the beginning of a rigorous understanding of value. This is where the innovation pipeline begins its dramatic slimming. Here, formal metrics are used for the first time to appraise the potential of proposed innovations. For example, a company might conclude that one idea has a market potential of $5 million and another has a $10 million potential. But that second idea may not launch until much later than the first. A third idea looks promising too, but the organization lacks the competencies to exploit it. What competencies will it need, and how can it get them? How does it begin prioritizing investments of time, people, and money?

Any idea that the organization advances to the next level of the pipeline enters the *development project portfolio*. This is where a flash of insight begins its transformation into a product and moves to the *launch portfolio*. In the *product portfolio*, an idea in development acquires the features and functions that will excite the market. Meanwhile, the road to market is being fully laid out.

PURSUE TRULY OPEN INNOVATION

Best Innovators are habitually and dramatically more collaborative at every point in the innovation process. We think we know why: they understand the limits of their resources and focus on what they do best. As Sun Microsystems co-founder Bill Joy famously remarked, "No matter who you are, most of the smartest people work for someone else."[19]

This phenomenon of open innovation is often touted as the coming move for companies that plan to boost their innovation programs. Best Innovators did that a while ago.

The Kapsch Group is one of Austria's leading technology companies, employing more than 5,000 people around the world. Georg Kapsch is its CEO. (He is also CEO of Kapsch TrafficCom.) What began as a manufacturer of telephones in 1892 has evolved to become a world-leading systems supplier for telecommunications and highway telematics. The company remains privately owned by Georg and his brother Kari, who is the COO. Notwithstanding the family's direct ownership, Kapsch Group has the too-familiar challenge of trying to remain leading edge even as it grows steadily larger and more far flung.

"The dilemma," observes Georg Kapsch, "is how to establish some form of organizational ambidexterity"—the capacity to attend to the core business with one hand while investigating future businesses with the other. Among the ways Kapsch has attempted to address the problem of ambidexterity is by pursuing innovation in collaboration with one of its many partners. Visit the Kapsch corporate website, for instance, and one of the first things you'll see is a list of the company's roughly 150 partners.

"It helps to get brains from outside the company," he says. "To share an idea, it's important to test it with different stakeholders or even someone from an analog market. The best ideas are generated in collaboration."

NETWORKS OF SMART PEOPLE

Collaborations outside the organization—of all kinds—are common among Best Innovators. Not surprisingly, award winners typically report that they generate more commercial successes from outside their organizations than non-winners.

Right now, Best Innovators may be ahead of the curve for the open-innovation phenomenon. Perhaps this is because their operational cultures tend to be inoculated against not-invented-here syndrome. Open innovation, however, is rapidly becoming so commonplace that soon it will hardly excite comment. This will be true for a number of reasons. The first is that all of us are used to living in a networked world, in both our personal and our working lives. We assume interconnectedness and question its absence.

The obvious causes of this cultural shift are the digital tools that accompany us everywhere we go, tools that are specifically designed to network across physical, organizational, and philosophical boundaries. These same tools have enabled legions of "smart people" to work independently of traditional organizations. But those traditional organizations haven't given up wanting smart people in their orbit.

The central reason open innovation is becoming a commonplace way of organizing innovation is that it works. It creates value from one end of the innovation portfolio to the other. Innovation metrics of all kinds are improved by the ability to draw on the combined capabilities of networks.

Partners in any collaboration meet where their interests converge. Considered another way, they are outsourcing activities at which they consider themselves inefficient. To raise overall innovation effectiveness and efficiency, they pool knowledge.

Based on its search fields, a large company might have an idea for a product. Involving partners in the development portfolio can lead to consideration of a diversity of approaches to a product's format—different ways of solving performance and function, each at a different cost, each requiring a different roadmap, perhaps using already available solutions. In this manner, product developers don't lock themselves into a single approach too early. This lowers their R&D budgets and reduces their innovation costs. Time to market can be markedly faster, and the success rate can be higher thanks to validating ideas with an external audience.

An open-innovation network can include one or several partners. In theory, there is no reason why even competitors can't be part of an open-innovation partnership. Barbara Dalibard of SNCF, who began her career at France Telecom in 1982, points out that so-called "co-opeting" among competitors is far from unknown in building large-scale telecommunications projects. She points to SNCF's collaboration with Deutsche Bahn to develop high-speed rail as an example of co-opeting in the railway industry.[20]

These kinds of collaborations have the potential to produce benefits for all parties by creating opportunities to share sources of value that cannot be easily traded or exchanged through arms-length arrangements. In 2014, the World Economic Forum (WEF) partnered with A.T. Kearney on an initiative called Fostering Innovation-Driven Entrepreneurship in Europe, undertaking extensive research including more than 60 structured interviews, eight high-level workshops, and a survey of more than 1,100 entrepreneurs and experts. An interesting result from the research are the positive outcomes of young firms and established companies collaborating to co-develop and take to market innovative ideas. Such collaborations represent a high-value, yet underutilized source of financial assets and network access for entrepreneurs. However, they also undoubtedly benefit large companies through the opportunity to participate in innovative activities.

The WEF's head of Europe, Nicholas Davis, argues that expanding this type of collaboration could significantly improve innovation ecosystems in Europe and around the world: "While collaborations between young start-ups and established businesses represent huge potential gains and are widely perceived as beneficial, they are inhibited by a lack of transparency and visibility of opportunities, weak cultures of collaboration, and the transaction costs of partnering," he says. "These can be overcome by entrepreneurs and companies having defined strategies, developing cultures of collaboration, and then focusing on carefully finding, attracting, negotiating, and executing partnerships."

The most common kinds of collaborations among Best Innovators are those with customers, suppliers, and universities. But they can include any player that stands to benefit from an affiliation with a partner that wants what they've got and from which they can borrow value.

For example, 3M takes a multipronged approach to creating value by leveraging strengths that include technology, manufacturing processes, a global footprint, and the 3M brand itself. Building the company's technology portfolio relies first on its R&D investments, with these internal efforts augmented by accessing external technology through M&A efforts and new ventures.

"We look for companies that can benefit from 3M's knowledge of how to develop, manufacture, and distribute solutions to a global customer base," says Jon Lindekugel, senior vice president of 3M Business Development. "We also look for companies led by high-energy, dynamic leaders who we are confident can carry their business plans forward successfully. Building a relationship based on synergy in all of these areas creates value in corporate venturing."

LINET is another good example. The Czech producer of high-end hospital beds is intensely interested in connecting with students. "Their advantage," says CEO Tomáš Kolář, "is that they are not restricted by operational blindness or auto-censorship when generating ideas. They sometimes come up with ideas that do not always make 100 percent sense," he says. "But after evaluation, a key attribute might be discovered to be a straight road to a full-scale innovation."

Medical technology firm QIAGEN follows the same objective in its bridge-building to research faculty. On a regular basis, the company holds a seminar for university scientists to present their newest work. All participants benefit from the exchange, and QIAGEN stays in the flow of new ideas.

In the next chapter, "Increase Innovation Efficiency and Speed," we look in depth at supplier partnerships. Managed correctly, supplier partnerships match customer collaborations as the most potent kinds of open innovation. But there are good reasons to be wary of embracing open innovation with too much freewheeling enthusiasm, whether with a supplier or anyone else. There is the risk of cyber attacks, the hazards of co-branding, patent litigations, and product liability responsibility, to name just a few. But these known risks can be managed.[21]

Success in any collaboration begins with being able to articulate how the partnership will support business strategy. Collaboration needs to be more than an avenue of cost reduction. For any party to a collaboration, the first job is knowing what capabilities it wants to access. All partners should be clear about the partnership model and know what optimal participation looks like: goals, responsibilities, margin model, organizational structure, interfaces, and process integration. There must be agreement on the long-term investment each partner will make in developing shared capabilities, such as staffing in support of coordination.

BOOST THE IDEA TRANSFER RATE

> "The innovation process is not static. It can always be adjusted if required."
>
> Gottfried Brunbauer
> CTO
> Rosenbauer

When measuring the success of an innovation portfolio, the key performance indicator is transfer rate. Transfer rate measures the ratio between the number of ideas from the time at which significant money has been invested in further development of the idea and the number of products or services that are launched in the market. A low transfer rate means a company is wasting money and time on too many duds. A high transfer rate means a company is efficient in its funnel management. Efficiency by itself does not assure success in the market. The time for assessing total return on innovation investment comes later.

"Our strength lies in our collection of ideas—their generation and their selection," says LINET CEO Tomáš Kolář. "In other words, in our decisions about which idea is elaborated upon as a priority, which is postponed, and which is abandoned altogether."

Transfer rate is not a measure of success for new products after they go to market. It only describes how many concepts survive the journey through the innovation funnel. Since no company has unlimited resources, the task for innovation managers is to establish selection criteria that ask the right questions about the contribution of a potential innovation before every step. Before a concept is allowed to move ahead, it must justify its right to exist.

An innovation portfolio evolves as it passes through a sequenced set of stage gates during which ideas grow steadily more concrete. The ideal at each gate is to distill the portfolio down to prospects with more measurable potential. The criteria for measuring potential are the same for each stage of a concept's progress through the pipeline:

* How attractive is the prospective market for the eventual product or service?
* What new customer value can the product or service create?
* What is the eventual product or service's likely competitive position?
* What is the concept's likely financial contribution?
* What effort is still needed to bring the eventual product or service to the market?

"The way from idea to product is regulated by a stage-gate process," says Gottfried Brunbauer, CTO of Rosenbauer, the Austrian giant in firefighting and civil-defense equipment. For example, he says, "We have a structured process to categorize new ideas. We start with a pragmatic categorization: is the idea completely new to us? Can it be a breakthrough innovation?" If the answers to these questions are yes, then Rosenbauer sets a next set of gates testing the business case for an innovation—prospective market appetite, patent research, a SWOT analysis (strengths, weaknesses, opportunities, and threats), expected time to market, and so on. At each stage of its movement through the company's portfolio, the business case is tested.

> *"If we want to grow major markets we have two options: gain market share or develop categories. To be really successful you should develop the category."*
>
> Bruno Piacenza
> EVP
> Henkel Laundry
> & Home Care

"All the decisions of the stage-gate process are documented in an idea database," Brunbauer says. "This ensures transparency of idea flows and process steps." In addition, he tracks important key performance indicators for productivity and activities in innovation management (a subject we take up in the next chapter). How long will it take, for example, until an idea reaches a specific status in its evolution? How long will it take for the idea to become a product?

"All these factors are included in a KPI matrix," says Brunbauer. "We chase the target internally with these KPIs to reduce idea lead times as much as possible. That lets us detect problems in every single process step so that steps can be taken. The innovation process is not static. It can always be adjusted if required."

Like Rosenbauer, German specialty chemicals company Evonik Industries AG is compelled by the multifaceted nature of its customer relationships to be adaptive in developing the value of its innovation pipeline—to be, in the words of Georg Kapsch, ambidextrous.

Evonik is, in a sense, a textbook example of how to use search fields to prime an innovation portfolio.

"As frameworks for innovation strategy," CEO Klaus Engel says, "search fields and competency portfolios can be mapped to align with growth targets outlined in our planning. Unfortunately, the tendency is to create these documents, file them away, and forget to apply their ideas to create real value."

A specialty producer like Evonik almost can't help having a full pipeline of innovation projects. In any given year, Evonik might be overseeing 500 initiatives among its business units or in its strategic research unit, Creavis, which was set up specifically to investigate potentially transformative innovations. These initiatives are incredibly diverse in scope, timeline, and the inputs required. For example, customers in the automotive industry expect new materials to undergo a long testing process. But in consumer goods, customers have to follow trends quickly; they have no time for extensive testing. Evonik doesn't have the luxury of viewing this as a dilemma. Its burden is managing its innovation portfolio with sufficient flexibility to address *all* the requirements of long, heavily documented projects and smaller quick-run projects.

To address this complexity, Evonik has developed an integrated portfolio management process called Idea to Profit (I2P). The process allows input from its search fields and its competency portfolio to flow into a database that steers new products across their entire lifespan. It uses checklists to turn ideas and inquiries into products and services. It offers tools for forced rankings and portfolio analyses. Additional features such as system-generated project reports and presentations reduce paperwork and improve the transfer rate.

Henkel Laundry & Home Care has also given a name to its portfolio-management tool. InnoGate was developed to optimize Henkel's innovation portfolio. Executive vice president Bruno Piacenza says InnoGate follows "the classic stage-gate system of concept definition, development, and validation phases." Concept generation, based on consumer need and subject to early winnowing, is the beginning.

Even among Best Innovators, Henkel distinguishes itself with a high number of best practices for portfolio optimization. The company persistently fosters its innovation culture with short- and long-term initiatives within and outside the organization—innovation challenges, competitions, and awards worldwide. Special emphasis is given to open innovation. Henkel has worked to systematize cross-industry innovation to improve product development and marketing concepts, intended to create business categories.

"If we want to grow major markets," says executive vice president Bruno Piacenza, "we have two options: gain market share or develop categories. To be truly successful, you should develop the category. This requires delivering innovations so the customer is willing to buy more or buy at a higher price."

Here's what this looks like in practice. In 2003, Henkel launched its first liquid rim block for toilets, the Duo-Active. It was an immediate success and soon accounted for more than 30 percent of annual sales in this product category.[22] By 2007, Henkel was looking forward to the rising curve of the Duo-Active life cycle while already working on its next rim block innovation.

The effort was in line with the innovation strategy of Laundry & Home Care. It would be bigger (to drive scale), better (to please consumers), and faster (rolling out within six months). The concept phase began with a multitalented team that included marketers, technical people from R&D, designers, and even advertising agencies.

The conventional value of a rim block is largely linked to hygiene. But a breakthrough innovation cannot only be about answering the market's known needs. In the development phase, the team explored unconventional trends for the toilet category: new shapes and designs. The bathroom, after all, is the one room in a home that guests are sure to visit. A rim block, the team believed, should not only be hygienic but should also offer other benefits.

After many attempts, the team came up with a design with four benefits: cleaning, anti-limescale, dirt removal, and freshness. The next challenge was the product launch.

The rim block, now called Power Active, was launched in mid-2010 and quickly rolled out to 50 countries. The launch was backed by a strategic communications plan reinforcing the message of the four benefits. In 2011, 47 million units were sold. In 2012, Power Active sales passed 120 million units. In less than two years, it became the fastest-growing category in Henkel's Laundry & Home Care business unit.

Bear in mind that the launch of Power Active came barely seven years after the very successful launch of Duo-Active. Henkel was using its InnoGate process to manage one product into maturity and another into birth.

In 2013, Laundry & Home Care reported that products less than three years old—innovations such as Power Active—accounted for 45 percent of the company's sales. The business unit looks to increase this to 50 percent.

This kind of aggressiveness is common among Best Innovators. 3M's NPVI figures have grown significantly and steadily over the past several years, and CEO Inge Thulin plans to see that continue. In 2014, 3M named a new head of research and development to reflect the company's conscious emphasis on gathering ideas from around the world to meet varying needs: Ashish Khandpur, who had been with 3M for nearly two decades. He brought to the position a strong background both in research science—Khandpur is an inventor on 10 issued patents—and time in business units and Asian subsidiaries.

"The culture in R&D at 3M is one of collaboration and sharing among our global technical community," he says. "We routinely build on each other's ideas in a boundary-less manner to solve the problems of our customers and to bring innovation to our global markets."

Khandpur oversaw the establishment of 3M's first full-fledged product development lab in India. There, customers prize "frugal and disruptive innovation," and 3M adopted its thinking accordingly. By its very nature, 3M focuses both on global megatrends as well as on opportunities that arise from local or regional trends.

Aggressive goals put an organization under enormous pressure that tests the strength of an innovation culture. It is also a test of the efficiency of an organization's processes, the subject we discuss in the next chapter.

BEST INNOVATORS DON'T DO IT ALONE

A Best Innovator's portfolio is complex and requires managing numerous and ever more sophisticated ideas toward commercial resolution. What gives this portfolio coherence is the rising expectation of viability as an idea advances down the narrowing funnel of the innovation portfolio. (As mentioned, the innovation portfolio is a funnel, where the many possibilities bubbling among search fields begin to be winnowed in favor of those with more promise of contributing to a balanced innovation strategy.) But Best Innovators don't do it alone.

At every point in the innovation process, Best Innovators are collaborative, especially in comparison to their industry peers. Best Innovators have been leading the way in developing best practice for open innovation for a long time. Perhaps this is because they understand the limits of their resources measured against the capabilities their innovation roadmaps show they need. So they focus on what they do best and borrow what they need from strategic partners—universities, consultancies, suppliers, and even competitors. Best Innovators are immune to the not-invented-here syndrome.

As we will discuss in chapter 6, "Improve Lifetime Profitability," Best Innovators are committed to their key performance indicators. Among their essential KPIs is transfer rate, which measures the relationship between the number of ideas in which money has been invested and the number of innovations actually realized. High transfer rates are the reward for aggressive goals. But aggressive goals test an innovator's ingenuity and flexibility, the subject we discuss in the next chapter, "Increase Innovation Efficiency and Speed."

INNOVATION MANAGEMENT IS CENTRAL TO ROSENBAUER'S APPROACH

In 1866, Johann Rosenbauer and some friends from the local gymnastics club in Linz started the city's first volunteer fire brigade. Johann sold basic firefighting equipment as a sideline. Later, his son Konrad took over as both commander of the volunteer firefighters and head of the business, which he expanded to include production of pumps and hoses. In the 1920s, Rosenbauer began manufacturing firefighting vehicles.

Fast-forward to the early 21st century. Rosenbauer is now the world leader in firefighting and civil-defense equipment. In 2012, it reported €645 million in revenue. Well more than half its 2,400 employees now work outside Austria. And still the tradition of volunteering in local fire brigades remains a staple of Rosenbauer's culture—in effect, turning employees into customers in addition to being good neighbors.

Rosenbauer CTO Gottfried Brunbauer calls this tradition *an essential advantage.* "It ensures us a multitude of ideas and inputs and makes the innovation process very efficient," he says. And it helps the company integrate customers into the innovation process.

One way Rosenbauer communicates its commitment to innovation is with its budget. In 2009, it invested €9.2 million in research and development. But when Rosenbauer won its Best Innovator award that year in the organization and culture category, it was not for its R&D spending. It was for what the judges called "systematic innovation management that includes all employees."

In 2012, Rosenbauer set up its Innovation, Technology, and Knowledge-Management Department. "Bundling these topics in one department offers us the best synergies," Brunbauer says. Although the effort is centralized, he refers to the department as a network.

Central to Rosenbauer's innovation-management process are teams in several locations that receive, evaluate, and consider development of new ideas.

More than a decade ago, Rosenbauer introduced a "contact group," a core of five or six people integrated in the Innovation, Technology, and Knowledge-Management Department and actively managing the innovation portfolio. The team consists of one or two full-time innovation coordinators and three or four employees on sabbatical from their regular work. The arrangement, says Brunbauer, assures broad expert knowledge and a rapid response to new ideas.

"We have products that are direct outcomes of our process that we wouldn't have without it," he says.

CROWDSOURCING INNOVATION

In 1795, the French government announced a prize for anyone who could solve the problem of preserving food for its army. Fifteen years later, the prize was awarded to Nicolas Appert for his method of conserving food in jars. We've been using refinements to Appert's method ever since. The French army, it turned out, crowdsourced a disruptive technology.

"Crowdsourcing" is a new word, largely because the digital tools that gave birth to the phenomenon are comparatively new. The coinage is usually attributed to Jeff Howe, an editor at *Wired* Magazine who first used the term in his 2006 article about the practice of outsourcing a problem to an anonymous network of people with an interest in its solution—the crowd.[23]

It makes sense for individual entrepreneurs with limited capabilities to crowdsource. It also makes sense for large organizations trying to gain access to the best thinking, no matter which direction it comes from, with the aim of grafting it onto their innovation culture.

In the past several years, the use of crowdsourcing as a tool of open innovation has jumped dramatically. In 2010, the number of completed crowdsourcing projects quintupled from the year before. In 2011, that number more than tripled. For now, at least, North America and Europe are the dominant practitioners of this type of open innovation, collectively hosting more than 90 percent of crowdsourced initiatives.

Crowdsourcing will accelerate at an even faster rate in the next few years. Big-data techniques will allow crowdsourcing without the direct participation of the crowd. It is already possible, for example, to translate hundreds of millions of tweets, a rich cacophony of unstructured data, into insights that can populate fertile search fields for new products and services. At the heart of this work is the ability to use machine-based computational linguistics to conduct sentiment analysis on a company's customers and its innovation portfolio. As we become better at big-data techniques, the impact on innovation portfolios will be profound.

Crowdsourcing initiatives often include some kind of compensation, such as prize money. Appert, for instance, won 12,000 francs. But for interested participants, the intellectual game and the pleasure of recognition may be more than enough reward.

Crowdsourcing has its risks, of course, not the least of which is being deluged with undeveloped ideas from all over the Internet. To help bring some order, so-called innovation brokerages have emerged in the past few years to act as intermediaries. It's a method some regard as imperfect but which has been used successfully by some Best Innovators, including Henkel Laundry & Home Care.

Step one of crowdsourcing: find the right crowd. Some kinds of questions are suitable for very open networks; others demand narrowly defined expert communities.

One of our clients solved that problem by restricting the definition of "the crowd" to inventors and graduate students. Simple filters allowed the company to quickly rate the most promising ideas. The highest-scoring participants were invited to a rapid refinement workshop at the company's headquarters. They were placed on teams with people from the company's marketing, finance, and R&D groups to assess the operational and financial feasibility of their ideas. The company obtained innovative ideas and capitalized on the experience to create an ongoing process for quickly filtering and refining ideas for future projects. It even hired a few graduate students.[24]

KAPSCH GROUP KEEPS AN EYE ON THE FUTURE

Kapsch Group is one of Austria's leading technology companies, with more than 5,000 employees around the world. Founded in 1892 as a manufacturer of telephones, it has become the world's leading system supplier for road-traffic telematics and telecommunications. The company is still privately owned, and brothers Georg and Kari Kapsch hold the positions of CEO and COO.

Typically, a Kapsch Group investment in new business must pass three tests: the new business must be global. It must be based on long-term trends. And it must be a niche that no other big player has entered—yet.

In recent years, Kapsch felt the bumps in the world economy, specifically in the government sector, where budget constraints led to decreases in project spending.

"A company can lose track rather quickly due to a lack of innovation," says Georg Kapsch. "The main innovation challenges are keeping up the culture and not getting satisfied in times of good results."

For an incumbent, that's an essential outlook.

"Threat comes from outside of your industry, not from within," he says. "The risk to incumbents is a threat discovered too late because the organization had its eye on the current core business—profitable today but without a market tomorrow."

With a nod to Joseph Schumpeter's theory of creative destruction, Kapsch points out that "innovation is not only about doing new things but about getting rid of traditional products, services, and companies. Otherwise, we could not afford to invest in new areas."

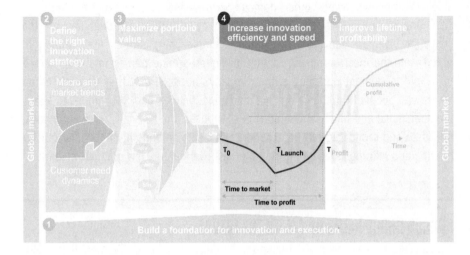

CHAPTER 5
INCREASE INNOVATION EFFICIENCY AND SPEED

Every great idea has a life cycle, from the glimmer of insight to its launch and finally to its eclipse by a new idea. Best Innovators understand that if they can't give an innovation eternal life, they at least have the power to expand how long it spends in the black by shortening its time to profit. Time to profit is the key performance indicator that, by focusing everyone on a common goal, drives cross-functional collaboration and breaks down barriers that too often exist among smart people inside—and outside—an organization. In this chapter we discuss the following topics:

- **Reduce time to profit.** Be aggressive in reducing time to market and time to profit. Time to profit is the decisive performance indicator, meaning: how long does it take for an idea to begin making money and earn the "innovation" title?

- **Manage the big metrics.** Read the performance of innovation strategies with attention to key performance indicators. KPIs create coherence in the strategy by painting a picture of how well an organization is aligned toward shared goals.

- **Treat interoperability as a decisive capability.** Drive cross-functional collaboration to decrease coordination efforts, prevent standalone solutions, and accelerate the overall innovation process.

- **Collaborate early with the right suppliers.** Supplier integration is a well-defined element of the innovation strategy. Strategic partners fill capability gaps, shorten time to market, elevate functionality, and reduce costs.

REDUCE TIME TO PROFIT

> *"We need to be able to apply high-quality competitive pressure, and compared to the competition, speed is our first advantage."*
>
> Jan Musil
> CEO
> ČKD

Speed matters. The faster an innovation gets to market, the more of its life cycle can be spent in the black. The Czech Republic's ČKD is a good example. With roughly 2,000 employees, the engineering firm is modest in size by international standards. But ČKD embraces that size as an advantage—one that gives it an edge not just for staying nimble but in how fast it can bring innovations to market.

"We need to be able to apply high-quality competitive pressure, and compared to the competition, speed is our first advantage," says CEO Jan Musil. "We're flexible. We make quick internal decisions, prepare a quality offer, validate it, and deliver it to the customer. Our processes are not overgrown," he says. "We adapt and react as a group."

ČKD works with a flexibility that may seem unavailable to its giant rivals. Functions within the company work in harmony to build new businesses. The firm works toward common ends with suppliers and stays close to customers to monitor their response to new ideas. And it can quickly get innovations to market.

However, such competencies have little to do with size.

MANAGE THE BIG METRICS

A few years ago, we worked with a mid-sized high-tech firm. The company's various commercial initiatives were managed by small teams, each responsible for different product lines. The performance of each team—and the compensation for each team's members—were assessed using time to profit.

For this company, time to profit was a strict measure that gave senior management the confidence to grant teams uncommon autonomy. Within a structure of clearly defined top-down guidelines, freedom was put in the hands of the people nearest the voice of the customer, closest to new ideas. Freedom enabled quick decisions, and quick decisions optimized time to profit. That was the KPI that teams used to measure success.

As a KPI, time to profit could not be more explicit in its meaning: how long does it take for an innovation to begin making money? This is not the same as time to market, which is the measure of how quickly an innovation moves out of the innovation portfolio and into the hands of customers. Time to market is important, but it is not the decisive KPI.

When we ask Best Innovators to measure their typical time to profit, we find that in comparison with their peers, they tend to be more deliberate and more aggressive in reducing both time to market and time to profit. The averages, of course, were calculated relative to specific industry life cycles; for example, smartphone makers contend with shorter life cycles than automobile manufacturers. Best Innovators estimate that 15 percent of their average product life cycle is spent bringing an innovation to market. For non-winners, the self-reported figure is 23 percent. But more revealingly, Best Innovators estimate that 28 percent of a product's life is spent getting to profitability. For non-winners, it's 39 percent.

What we observe among Best Innovators is not simply that they have shorter time to market and shorter time to profit—they are persistently better than their peers in these measures (see figure 6). We think this is because Best Innovators are more committed to achieving their key performance indicators.

For Best Innovators, the logic of managing by KPIs is obvious: if you don't rigorously measure performance, how do you read the performance of your innovation strategy? Without rigorous adherence to the stories, KPIs cannot identify that the view into an innovation portfolio is cloudy.

Figure 6

Best Innovators use cross-functional KPIs to encourage collaboration

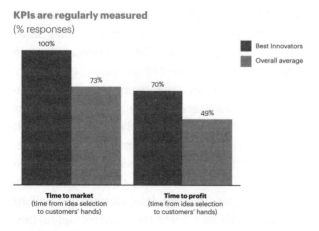

KPIs are regularly measured
(% responses)

- Best Innovators
- Overall average

Time to market
(time from idea selection
to customers' hands)

Time to profit
(time from idea selection
to customers' hands)

Source: A.T. Kearney Best Innovator Competition

LINET, the Czech maker of smart hospital beds, may be typical of Best Innovators in its grasp of what Rosenbauer CTO Gottfried Brunbauer calls "the KPI matrix." LINET CEO Tomáš Kolář knows his company's average time to market and time to profit off the top of his head. "In fiscal 2013, average time in development was 15 months," he says. "We reach profitability in 39 months from product launch. The average life cycle of key products is seven and a half years."

For LINET, KPIs are more than a retrospective accounting of a completed initiative. They are a guide to operational improvement. As Kolář points out, they give LINET "control of our assumptions for planning and monitoring in-novation projects. These parameters can be steadily improved." LINET is intent on shortening the development cycle of its beds from 22 months down to nine.

Whirlpool, the appliance giant that won a 2010 Best Innovator award for its Brazilian operation, is distinguished in its management by KPIs. Before start-ing what it calls "the innovation embedment approach" 20 years ago, average sales values were declining by about 2 percent every year. For the past 10 years, there has been a precise reversal of that trend, with prices climbing on average 2 percent in aggregate. The root of this improvement was the closely measured development of new products and incremental innovations.

Whirlpool's portfolio of products classified as innovative are responsible for one-fourth of its Latin American revenue. They are on average two to three times more profitable than the rest of its product portfolio.

THE BIRTH OF NPVI

3M uses a measurement known as the New Product Vitality Index (NPVI) to measure its innovation portfolio. As a KPI, it is more precise than time to market in its reliance on reported quarter-to-quarter performance numbers. In 3M's case, NPVI measures revenue derived from innovations introduced within the past five years as a percent of total sales.

Other companies have adapted NPVI to measure the success of their own innova-tion strategies. Variation is typically around how they define "new." Does a product exten-sion count as new? And how *new* is *new* anyway? Henkel Laundry & Home Care defines its sales from products introduced in the past three years as a percentage of net sales.

"The only good measure of innovation is the amount of orders and profit generat-ed by innovative products," says Valeo CEO Jacques Aschenbroich. "Around 30 percent of our order intake is generated by new products, which are more profitable than the average. We also use additional indicators to manage innovation—patents, for instance. Filing patents aims at protecting our innovation and increasing its value," he says, "and is not an objective per se." Independent industry awards can also be a marker of how innovative a company is. Valeo, for example, was awarded four Automotive News PACE Awards over the past three years: one in 2014 for its back-over protection system; two in 2013 for its air intake module, including an award for the best innovation partnership with an original equipment manufacturer, Volkswagen; and one in 2012 for its Aqua Blade wiper system.

Whichever timeframe a company chooses, the virtue of an NPVI-like measure is that it uses hard data to give the clearest visibility into the progress of an innovation portfolio.

Whirlpool's management of its innovation portfolio begins even before an idea is added to its search fields. Before any concept can be investigated as an innovation, it must pass three tests: is it potentially compelling to Whirlpool customers? Is it aligned to Whirlpool brands? Does it create sustainable value for Whirlpool shareholders? From there, things get much more concrete, and that concreteness is measured by KPIs.

Whirlpool has three essential metrics of an innovation's progress toward profitability, all of them bearing directly on the evolution of the innovation portfolio:

- **iFunnel** is the estimated steady-state revenue of active projects. It monitors the early-stage process of generating and then developing innovative ideas.

- **iPipe** is steady-state revenue. It is related to product and solution development.

- **iRevenue** is the actual revenue of products and solutions already in the market and their end-of-production lift.

Whirlpool makes its KPI matrix literally visible each month when the output of these metrics is displayed on its innovation dashboard, which allows the company to look at the matrix of its KPIs in their totality, by region, and by major product category. The dashboard also takes the pulse of its progress,

> *"A product that is ready to be marketed is always the result of a successful cooperation among partners across the value chain."*
>
> Peer Schatz
> CEO
> QIAGEN

establishing benchmarks and allowing the organization to make fact-based decisions on a number of dimensions about its investment in innovation.

Whirlpool's rigor is made necessary by the generally mature and saturated nature of its core business of home appliances. In such a context, it will always be difficult to make the business case for a new product. Not surprisingly, a look at Whirlpool's innovation portfolio reveals that more of its successful innovation initiatives emerge from opportunities that either expand the company's core business or go beyond it.

Best Innovators adhere to their KPIs because they work. They create coherence in an innovation strategy by painting a clear picture of how well the whole organization is aligned toward the same goals.

TREAT INTEROPERABILITY AS A DECISIVE CAPABILITY

KPIs improve interoperability, a term we borrowed from the language of systems engineering. It alludes to the degree of interaction among different elements in a system. Individual elements within an interoperable system collaborate in support of the whole and, when the need arises, can be borrowed for parts to support the work of other elements. An interoperable innovation system might share knowledge; it might even share budget and time. Most of all, it shares the talent of the organization in support of new endeavors.

A.T. Kearney's definition of interoperability emphasizes this boundary-crossing aspect. Interoperability is the glue that holds an innovative organization together. Or as QIAGEN CEO Peer Schatz describes it, "Within the company, we link all organizational units and processes to innovation. A product that is ready to be marketed is always the result of a successful cooperation among partners across the value chain."

Consider an organization along two dimensions: functional excellence and cross-functional collaboration. In the 21st century, functional excellence is generally quite high, particularly in large organizations. Modern corporations are generally outstanding in the way they manage purchasing, manufacturing, engineering, sales and marketing, and after-sales support. There are multiple best practice models, many well-described stages of excellence, and plenty of experiences to draw upon.

However, cross-functional excellence is another matter. Cross-functional collaboration can be a decisive capability, and yet unlike expertise in managing individual functions, the literature of cross-functional excellence—interoperability—is pretty thin.

One company we worked with had top products, an excellent brand, and world-class sales management, but it was cannibalizing its product lines and beginning to have serious problems in customer service. Within the company, cross-functional excellence was not even discussed. But we can cite many examples of Best Innovator teams that worked across functions. In each instance, the innovation emerging from the teams was not regarded as an achievement owned by R&D or design or marketing but by all the collaborators in the network.

Some companies are more formal in the ways they organize cross-functional collaboration. Consider Coca-Cola.

> *"The ability to identify a latent demand and a new product requires managing innovation in a holistic way across all parts of the value chain."*
>
> Ravi Kant
> Former Vice Chairman
> Tata Motors

"Over the past few years, we've been building multiple platforms of subject-matter experts around the world," says Coke's chief technology officer, Guy Wollaert. "We created an app that makes these networks visible. Press a button, and our global engineering network comes up visually, with all its information." A pod on such a network might be in Japan, for instance. Coke's application will pull up the names and numbers of the managers, experts, and functional expertise. The nice thing about this, Wollaert says, is that "you don't need to be the person who knows everybody anymore. You have transparency from the first move onward. It's how we make all our networks accessible to everyone in the system." What is too clear to be ignored, he says, is that "the speed of innovation has to accelerate. This is where technology helps and where you need those internal networks. If you do not rely on them, things get stuck."

Similarly, German restaurant-equipment maker Rational employs more than 300 master chefs in sales, research, and customer consulting who also work in close contact with the company's engineers in product development. Their collaboration is what Valeo CEO Jacques Aschenbroich calls the "network of experts" inside his company. Members of the network are responsible not just for continually developing their own competencies but for transmitting their knowledge to other corners of the organization. To keep the network dynamic, the members of the network must be periodically reconfirmed. "For our engineers, this is an important recognition step," Aschenbroich says.

When measuring the productivity of this kind of cross-functional collaboration, it helps to start with elements that are hard to measure, namely the "soft" culture stuff that Best Innovators tend to get right—elements such as a clear perspective on the future and sustained attention on what it takes to get there, from an environment that gives talented people room to excel and excites real passion for work to a senior team that leads by example in sharing information and fostering collaboration.

KPIs can drive more concrete measures of interoperability. In one recent case, the performance of a networked team was evaluated by time to profit, a cross-functional KPI measuring a cross-functional capability. (In this case, senior management's seriousness about interoperability was further measured by a team bonus, shared equally among the team members—a further incentive for cross-functional teamwork.)

"The ability to identify a latent demand and a new product," observes former Tata Motors vice chairman Ravi Kant, "requires managing innovation in a holistic way across all parts of the value chain."

Kant is referring to Tata's Ace, the light truck that gave birth to a successful new vehicle line after its launch in 2005. Ace was the fruit of a cross-functional Tata team's collaboration. The team's first move was to fan out across rural and urban India to interview drivers of nearly 4,000 three-wheel cars and trucks—the so-called "auto rickshaws" so common throughout the country. The team discovered an appetite for a light truck that would be fuel efficient, safe, cheap, and status-enhancing.

From the outset, Tata's product development focused on high-speed innovation and faster time to profit. The lead team had five full-time members and the support of 400 other professionals inside Tata, as well as what Kant calls "regular mentoring" by senior leadership. The team took a "target cost" approach, committing to a price tag of a little more than $2,000 for the new vehicle. Factor costs would have to support that target, and that could only be done with the collaboration of all of Tata's functions.

Within months of the launch of the two-cylinder Ace, production capacity doubled from 30,000 to 60,000 units a year, and a new factory was built in Pantnagar with an annual capacity of 250,000 units. Tata had created a new segment in the Indian automotive industry and inspired new competitors to enter the segment. Of even more enduring impact, lessons learned from the Ace project gave Tata's other innovation efforts a new rigor.

"Ace was a quantum leap in our approach to innovation management," Kant says. "Processes and structural enhancements introduced during the Ace project have since been institutionalized." These include market studies, voice-of-customer assessments, and a five-stage-gate system. Evaluation of ideas in Tata's innovation portfolio now draws heavily on summaries of market opportunity, product concepts, the business case, and the investment required.

Meanwhile, cross-functional teams have become the norm for Tata's innovation efforts. The teams are given well-defined targets in terms of development, quality, and cost—all with the goal of cutting time to market and time to profit.

COLLABORATE EARLY WITH THE RIGHT SUPPLIERS

Before the Ace trucks, innovation at Tata Motors was characterized by vertical integration. Among the process changes Tata institutionalized in the past five or 10 years has been a far greater openness to external collaborators, specifically its suppliers.

Supplier innovation is a hot topic among senior managers, and for good reasons.[25] High-growth companies know they can't do it alone, or at least not for very long. One way to bridge the gap between big ambitions and deficiencies in capabilities is to *borrow* what the organization needs from suppliers that may be further along a given technology curve than even the most talented incumbent.

Suppliers can relieve some of the intense cost pressure associated with research and development, the expense of which tends to grow faster than sales. That translates into faster time to profit. However, Best Innovators have learned that partnering with suppliers is not only about outsourcing costs (see figure 7).

Among Best Innovators, supplier integration has emerged as a well-defined element of business strategy. (Part of the reason for this may be that Best Innovators assume that unending business-model innovation is a natural state.) Valeo, for example, developed its Five Axes methodology to focus every aspect of the enterprise on operational excellence. The Five Axes are constant innovation, total quality, production system, involvement of personnel, and supplier integration. Perhaps because Valeo is a strategic supplier to the world's automotive industry, it knows how essential suppliers can be to maximizing the profitability of an innovation.

The Five Axes is part KPI matrix, part process chart, and part handbook to an innovation culture. In this methodology, cross-functional collaboration is implicit. Perhaps by extension of this openness, Valeo developed a markedly active approach to supplier integration.

As an organization, Valeo can be described as a constellation of cross-functional project teams simultaneously engineering products and processes. Reducing manufacturing complexity—and lowering costs—are preoccupations for

Figure 7

Best Innovators partner with suppliers early and not only to cut costs

Main reason for early supplier involvement
(% responses[1])

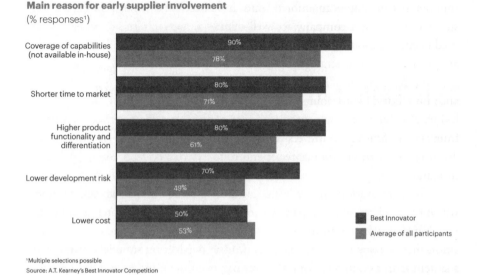

Coverage of capabilities (not available in-house)	90% / 78%
Shorter time to market	80% / 71%
Higher product functionality and differentiation	80% / 61%
Lower development risk	70% / 49%
Lower cost	50% / 53%

■ Best Innovator
■ Average of all participants

[1] Multiple selections possible
Source: A.T. Kearney's Best Innovator Competition

these teams. That's where supplier partnerships come in. Valeo looks to suppliers to be genuine collaborators in what it calls the Constant Innovation Axis. Suppliers work side by side with Valeo project teams to develop productivity plans and quality improvements and are co-creating key technologies.

The suppliers that Valeo has established these close partnerships with are an elite group with which the company maintains mutually beneficial long-term relationships. They are Valeo Integrated Partners, or VIPs—"the best in the world," says CEO Jacques Aschenbroich.

"Open innovation is increasingly important in the automotive industry," he says, "and our innovation process ensures access to intelligence wherever it sits."

In the generation of new ideas, open innovation may involve partners from every point on the compass, not just suppliers. Valeo has built successful partnerships with all kinds of collaborators, including universities, start-ups (developing an electric supercharger, for example), and large companies (collaborating with France-based Safran on self-driving solutions for automobiles, military vehicles, and aircraft).

Integrating select suppliers into the innovation process, though, is another category of collaboration. Strategic suppliers are part of an ongoing partnership that can fill skills gaps, shorten time to market, elevate functionality, and reduce costs. If the organizational culture allows it to happen, supplier partnerships can inform innovation strategy, enabling a company to make clear-eyed decisions about how it defines what is in and what is out of its strategic core.

> *"Our innovation process ensures access to intelligence wherever it sits."*
>
> Jacques Aschenbroich
> CEO
> Valeo

As the CEO of Whirlpool Brazil's appliance unit Enrico Zito points out, "Becoming less able to fully develop a product internally from start to finish is an irreversible tendency." To meet ever-shorter product cycles and time-to-market requirements, he says, Whirlpool engages and "contaminates" suppliers with its innovation process. A good example is Whirlpool's new oven design, which relies on customer sensors and resistors developed by a strategic supplier.

Or consider the evolution of supplier relationships at Coca-Cola, a transition that has opened up the organization of what has historically been "more a system than a company," in the words of CTO Guy Wollaert. Since its beginnings in the 1880s, Coke's system has always been an intimate set of collaborative relationships within a network of strategic suppliers and bottlers around the world.

Coke's route to becoming a $47 billion international brand "relies more on innovation than M&A," Wollaert says. Most of these innovations have been incremental. Coke's marketing innovations are numerous, including the pioneering use of coupons in the early years of the 20th century. The company has also been willing to experiment with its core brand, whether it's tinkering with container designs or introducing the Diet Coke portfolio in the 1970s.

Coke has also pursued disruptive innovation outside its core business of soft drinks. Wollaert points out that although disruptive change gets less attention in the company's innovation portfolio than incremental change (the kind likely to be strongly backed by marketing departments), when they do happen, disruptions induce step change and high value.

In the 1990s, for example, Coke was the first to bottle juice drinks with pulp, an initiative that became a billion-dollar business in just a few years. In 2005, the company introduced Coke Zero, a low-calorie drink aimed at men, and in a few years, it too was earning billions in revenue. In 2010, Coke introduced its Freestyle machines, a touch-screen "soda fountain" that allows users to customize more than 100 Coca-Cola products with a menu of flavors.

> "Becoming less able to fully develop a product internally from start to finish is an irreversible tendency."
>
> Enrico Zito
> CEO, appliance unit
> Whirlpool Brazil

Coke built its Freestyle machine in collaboration with suppliers outside its conventional network. The machine's cabinet was designed by Italy's Pininfarina, which made its reputation working with automotive companies such as Ferrari. The soul of the new machine, its PurePour system, is an adaption of micro-dispensing technologies used to deliver precise dosages of drugs to cancer patients.[26]

"Historically," says Wollaert, "we have primarily been innovating 'inside-in.' With all the partners we have—suppliers, customers, bottlers—we've innovated from within. That's been our ecosystem. But as a result of exploring totally different partners we had no relationship with before, we see opportunities—new frameworks, new business models, new ways to handle IT, new ways to compensate people that work and develop for us. And that requires new ecosystems." Coke even has a name for this new ecosystem: the Global Technical and Engineering Community, a platform for connecting talent with need across business units.

Wollaert expects Freestyle to be a disruptive innovation not just for the soft-drink business but for Coke, beginning with its bottling system.

However, just like the subject of open innovation, many companies talk about supplier integration, but not enough know how to manage it well. Part of the problem is a natural ambivalence about having an intimate relationship with an external party. As one Best Innovator, a well-known practitioner of open innovation, says warily, "In principle, I see open innovation with suppliers as critical. But tier 1 suppliers are also serving other competitors. It is hard to rely on sustainable competitive advantage coming out of that kind of innovation process."

Certainly, leakage of intellectual property is high on the list of reasons why many companies are leery of full partnership with suppliers. Also high on the list of concerns is the difficulty in aligning an outsider with an organization's long-term innovation roadmap and the risk of picking the wrong supplier as a strategic partner.

For Best Innovators, the first step toward dealing with these concerns (and constructing durable supplier partnerships) is involving the procurement function right from the beginning of a product's life cycle—at the wide end of the innovation funnel (see figure 8).

Figure 8

The earlier suppliers are involved, the greater the potential impact on life-cycle costs

Life-cycle costs

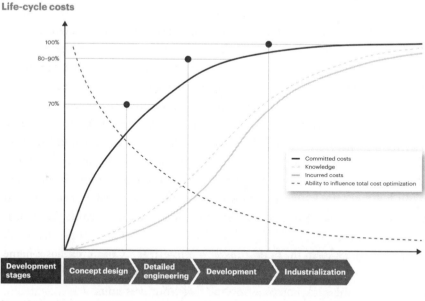

Source: A.T. Kearney Best Innovator Competition

The problem here is that non-winners' procurement functions typically lack the influence of, say, sales or engineering. The principal role of procurement is viewed as getting a good price on materials and not much more. The driver of product development tends to be the engineering function. In that role, it often specifies what it wants in a product, which is quite often the same thing as choosing the same suppliers that engineers have been comfortable with for a long time but which might not be the best fit as strategic partners. As a result, procurement enters the conversation too late to shape the discussion about supplier partnerships in the best way. That's a loss to the innovation process.

But consider this: in 2011, A.T. Kearney surveyed procurement and supply-chain executives at 185 companies in 32 industries to get their measure of "excellence" in procurement. The study found that the leaders used supplier-relationship management processes more consistently than their peers. Ninety percent reported that their companies had increased procurement's role in developing and executing business strategies. Three-quarters said collaborations with vendors contributed to innovation by integrating suppliers into the new-product development process, reducing time to market for new products and creating business opportunities. Moreover, the leaders were twice as likely to use the procurement function to increase the total value of purchased goods, build synergies across business units, and improve working capital.[27]

Best Innovators are shifting their thinking about the procurement from "cost out" to "profit improvement." Procurement has, or should have, up-close intelligence on suppliers that no other function owns. For example, procurement might conduct a supplier scan during an idea's development phase. This can take the organization beyond its known supplier base—a supplier base so familiar that all concerned may no longer bring fresh eyes to the relationship. As Coca-Cola has discovered, suppliers from outside an industry can offer a new perspective on engineering—a new insight into functionality, perhaps, or a different point of view about product formulation. Or again, consider Whirlpool, which invests heavily in building strategic partnerships with suppliers identified as trendsetters in the application of materials, regardless of the industries with which they're normally associated.

We have explored the opportunities of supplier innovation management assessment together with the customer's procurement department. The outcome of this structured workshop based on the IMP³rove assessment was enlightening both for the strategic supplier and the customer's procurement department. It was the first time the supplier had the chance to discuss innovation-related topics with its customer while at the same time gaining insights about benchmarks on its innovation management capabilities. For the first time, the customer's procurement department understood the innovation management system that the supplier had put in place and the solution capability they had developed for challenges the customer had struggled with for a long time.

KPIs are a preoccupation for Best Innovators, and the decisive KPI is time to profit. The faster an innovation gets to market and begins earning back the money invested in it, the more of its life cycle can be spent in the black.

Focusing on time to profit clarifies the other choices Best Innovators make. It allows managers, for instance, the confidence to grant their teams the autonomy and power to make decisions. Quick decisions optimize time to profit. The sequence is that direct.

For Best Innovators, the logic of managing by KPIs is obvious: if the performance of their innovation portfolios isn't measured, then how will they know if their strategy is working? KPIs, in that respect, look not backward but forward toward operational improvement. They are shared measures of success understandable to the whole organization. For example, KPIs enable performance measures for cross-functional collaborations by giving attention to outcomes and not to which function gets how much credit for a successful innovation.

Best Innovators have learned to regard collaborative ability as a decisive capability. Their organizations create the conditions for talented people to shine and to work with passion toward a shared goal. They promote an organizational psychology that responds well to external collaborations, particularly the strategic supplier collaborations that can contribute so much to every facet of an innovation effort.

Best Innovators know they can't do it alone. External partners—suppliers in particular—are crucial to filling the gaps between the big ambitions and the missing capabilities needed to realize them. The goal is still the same: faster time to profit.

WHAT DO YOU KNOW?

Knowledge is an innovation competency. Sharing knowledge is an innovation capability. At the end of a product's life cycle, sharing knowledge will have been the source of the value created by cross-functional teams. In the words of Barbara Dalibard of SNCF Voyages, sharing knowledge "hustles our habits."

Knowledge management was a vogue term in the 1990s. Since then, the term has been treated with some skepticism by many organizations that spent serious money building knowledge management systems without being able to say precisely what they got for their investment.

In a prescient *Harvard Business Review* essay more than 20 years ago, Tom Davenport, one of the discipline's early proponents, saw the roots of eventual disappointment with knowledge management:

> Information technology has a polarizing effect on managers; it either bedazzles or frightens. Those who are afraid of it shun it, while bedazzled IT departments frequently become prisoners of their own fascination, constructing elaborate technology architectures and enterprise information models to guide systems development. Senior executives who buy into this view promote technology as the key catalyst of business change. But such technocratic solutions often specify the minutiae of machinery while disregarding how people in organizations actually go about acquiring, sharing, and making use of information.[28]

QIAGEN begins with what Davenport called "the human dimension" in its approach to knowledge sharing among cross-functional teams. CEO Peer Schatz says QIAGEN actively links learning and working processes with one another. To keep pace with the day-to-day expansion of intelligence—within the company and out in the world at large—QIAGEN built an online library to ensure transparency into the development of the organization's knowledge base. Current research results and solutions, for example, are accessible to every employee.

"Like any other company, there is an external dynamic in the industry outside our organization," says Schatz. "That has to be reflected in our internal dynamic, particularly with respect to speed. The integration of the entire environment in the innovation process gives a new impulse for the development of ideas."

LINET seeks to capture the external dynamic in its "department for protection of intellectual property." The department was conceived as a central piece of LINET's innovation program. Its mission is monitoring the activities of competitors and identifying possibilities for achieving the same results without violating the intellectual-property rights of competitors. This approach generates new product initiatives about a third of the time. The department also provides regular technology updates and evaluates LINET's own innovation initiatives for their risk of actual or future solution redundancy. The potential of any new initiative is further evaluated from the view of what LINET executive director Tomáš Kolář calls "patentability."

Austrian firefighting-equipment maker Rosenbauer consolidates its intelligence under the unambiguous headings of innovation, technology, and knowledge.

"Bundling these in one department offers us the best synergies," says CTO Gottfried Brunbauer. "It involves as many employees as possible and offers us fundamental support during the innovation process."

VALEO IS A CONSTANT INNOVATOR

Innovation is woven into the fabric of Valeo's culture. Along with total quality, supplier integration, production systems, and involvement of personnel, constant innovation is an integral part of the company's Five Axes methodology, which focuses every part of the enterprise on operational excellence.

In 2007, Valeo was recognized for the success of its methods and process management with France's Best Innovator award. The firm is one of the world's leading automotive suppliers—a €12.1 billion designer, producer, and seller of components, integrated systems, and modules for cars and trucks. The company has 123 plants, 16 research centers, 34 development centers, and 12 distribution platforms in 29 countries worldwide. Among its 78,600 employees, nearly 10,000 are dedicated to research and development. In 2013, Valeo's total R&D effort amounted to €1.1 billion—about 10 percent of original equipment sales and 50 percent more than in 2009.

To this distributed team of innovators, the Constant Innovation policy gives structure to research and innovation processes all the way through to product launch.

Valeo credits the Constant Innovation effort with the development and successful launch of its innovations, including the integrated Starter Alternator Reversible System (iS-tARS). This belt-driven starter-alternator reduces the fuel consumption of combustion engines by up to 15 percent in congested city driving. "In the city, a car is idle about 35 percent of the time," says Derek de Bono, Valeo's marketing director. "Making engines shut down and restart automatically is an easy, affordable solution to reducing vehicle CO_2 emission and improving fuel economy."[29]

COCA-COLA: A WORLD LEADER GROUNDED IN INNOVATION

Coca-Cola didn't set out to be in the soft-drinks business. The inventor of its core product, John Stith Pemberton, thought he was inventing a "brain tonic" when he created his "cocoa wine" in 1886. He could never have imagined that one day there would be anything like Coke Zero. Or that the business he started in his pharmacy would generate revenue of $47 billion a year from around the world.

Originally, Coke's core business was syrup production, which it sent out to local pharmacies as a treatment for everything from headaches to exhaustion. In 1889, the company introduced its franchised distribution system, selling Coca-Cola syrup to a network of bottlers around the world. As early as 1917, there was a Coke bottler on the island of Guam.

From its beginnings, Coke has been built on an extended network of bottlers and suppliers with a distributed innovation strategy. The famous design of the Coca-Cola bottle, for example, was devised in Indiana in 1915 and then modified by bottlers to suit the needs of production lines.

By the 1950s, a third of Coke's revenue was coming from international markets. Coke's first product innovation came from a foreign market: Fanta Orange was created in Naples, Italy, in 1955 and was not sold in the United States until 1960, the same year Coke entered the fruit juice business with its acquisition of Minute Maid.

Coke had an ironic sort of "failure" when New Coke was introduced in 1985. The update on the classic Coke formula was intended to appeal to what research determined was a growing customer taste for sweeter soft drinks (like those made by its rival, Pepsi Cola). New Coke is remembered now not as a daring innovation but as a marketing blunder. Sales were strong, but an intense minority of loyalists to the classic formula pressured local bottlers, which passed along their grievances to Coke. The company knew enough to fail fast. Seventy-nine days after New Coke's introduction, Classic Coke returned. Sales soared, leading some to suggest it had been a marketing gimmick all along. It wasn't.

Even Roger Enrico, Pepsi's CEO at the time, applauded Coca-Cola's support for the team that took the risk with New Coke. "To fire them because of one mistake—no matter how huge—is to put everyone who works at Coke on notice," he said. "One slip, and you're out. That wouldn't yield better performance. It would only eliminate all risk taking."[30]

Coke's CTO Guy Wollaert says, "We want to be recognized again as the preeminent entrepreneurial company in the food and beverage industry. I say 'again' because the Coca-Cola Company would not have been what it's become if it didn't have remarkable successes from innovation. The product itself has been an example of disruptive innovation. It was something new to the world."

INTEROPERABILITY IS A REQUIREMENT AT ČKD GROUP

Českomoravská Kolben-Daněk (ČKD) traces its roots back to 1927, when the combination of two small Czech firms produced an innovative four-stroke engine, turbine, and generators. ČKD long ago left the engine business and was for generations one of the world's leading builders of tram cars and gas and oil technologies, most of which went to Soviet bloc countries during the Cold War years.

ČKD's old businesses struggled to find their way in the post-Soviet era. By the end of the 1990s, however, the company had already begun its transformation into ČKD Group, an engineering and production company with interests in power generation, gas and oil, environmental technologies, and infrastructure development.

All of ČKD's businesses are built on inventories of competencies. The group's senior management is explicit in its desire for interoperability among these competencies across the holding-company structure. Market pressure for simultaneous technical innovation and lower costs is unrelenting, especially for a comparatively small firm such as ČKD.

ČKD has a long tradition of working with suppliers that contribute services and tools the group might lack in their inventories of competencies. For customers, supplier alliances bring speed and better reliability. For ČKD, they reduce R&D costs and accelerate time to market—the latter a key performance indicator within ČKD. A strict rule within the group is that time to market for any new product or service emerging from one of the ČKD companies cannot be longer than 36 months.

Creating a coherent innovation strategy among these internal and external partnerships depends on talent.

"Experience is always welcome," says CEO Jan Musil. "But creativity and the ability to link seemingly unconnected things is a gift—a gift that can be cultivated by the right leadership."

LINET'S GAMBLE ON INNOVATION PAYS OFF

Since its launch in 1990, LINET has been making hospital beds in the Czech city of Želevčice u Slaného. By 1995, 150 people were building about 3,000 beds a year.

LINET might have continued on that scale for a long time, enjoying the price advantage of producing in a low-wage market. But in the late 1990s, the company made a bet on innovation. Fifteen years later, it was producing 40,000 beds a year and employing 600 people.

LINET may have had low-cost advantages, but it also had low brand awareness in the world's medical markets—and it carried the stigma of being a post-communist enterprise. The breakthrough came in 1999 when LINET patented the linear column unit, redefining the technology of electronically adjustable beds and establishing the company as an innovator in the industry.

Today, LINET is one of the world's four largest producers of hospital beds, reporting more than €127 million in 2012 and 2013. Nearly all of that—more than 90 percent—was generated by export. LINET maintains an actively managed innovation portfolio. Within the same two-year period, products younger than three years old brought in almost half of the company's sales. The time from first appraisal of an idea until the launch of a new product averaged about 22 months—until 2012, when time to market dropped to 15 months. LINET now aims to get that down to nine months. Time to profit averages 39 months or better—a healthy ratio in an industry where the lifespan of key products is seven and a half years.

"Our strength lies in the collection of ideas," says CEO Tomáš Kolář, "not just in their generation but in our decisions about which to make a priority, which to postpone, and which to abandon."

To make these decisions, LINET works closely with medical professionals, whose knowledge is crucial to creating competitive advantage in a product that, as Kolář points out, "on first look may seem exactly the same as our competitors."

Such open innovation has been characteristic of LINET since its breakout in the late 1990s, including input by customers and strategic suppliers. Customer experiences—even the negative ones—can be invaluable spurs to product innovation. LINET estimates that half the ideas in its innovation portfolio are customer generated—more than double the number derived from patent searches and internal brainstorms.

"Around the world, significant shifts are occurring in the accessibility of medical technology," Kolář says. "It's become mobile, and that's been a big change lever in many industries, including ours. We've seen a large number of new competitors enter our markets. Innovation is going to be absolutely key for us—and our biggest competitive advantage."

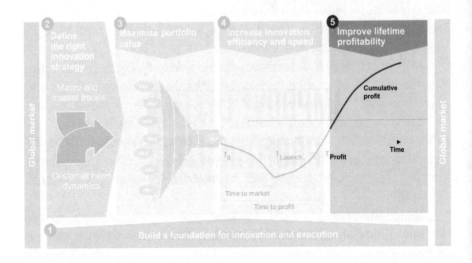

CHAPTER 6
IMPROVE LIFETIME PROFITABILITY

Making innovation a repeatable process is never about relying on lightning strikes of insight or the individual genius of one leader. On the contrary, we have described many ways Best Innovators make their entire operations superior. In this chapter, we show how Best Innovators secure or even improve profitability over the entire product or service life cycle. We talk about:

- **Ensure process coherence.** See processes as part of a whole, as components in a machine that generates new products, services, and business models—sustaining the innovation advantage by attaining ever-better levels of process efficiency.

- **Manage complexity.** Focus less on reducing complexity than on managing it coherently. Managed correctly, complexity creates a rationale for premium prices and the higher profitability those prices deliver.

- **Leverage agile and lean design.** Take traditional "lean design" to a new level, often called "design to cost." The focus is on core functionality, the central job a product or service does for customers. This yields uncommonly transparent views into core factor costs and a blueprint for design.

- **Further improve interoperability and collaborative partnerships.** Be cross-functional by habit and intention. This expansive view of collaboration carries over to relationships to further reduce costs, generate ideas, and develop implementation processes.

ENSURE PROCESS COHERENCE

In every age, the need for efficiency and profitability is always intense but never more so than in the current era, especially for incumbents. The returns from investing in continuous improvement processes are diminishing while the cost-reduction opportunities to be had by sourcing globally are slowly being exhausted. Although incumbents will continue to grow their presence in foreign markets, it will be for new reasons: proximity to customers and customizing products to local markets. Meanwhile, the same countries from which incumbent companies once sourced cheap materials and labor are becoming the next generation of competitors.

"The local market of our Chinese competitor is by far bigger and growing faster than our local ones in Europe," observes one Best Innovator well-known for building international supplier partnerships. Within a generation, Chinese companies will probably be telling a similar tale.

The answer to sustainable growth in the coming era—both for established innovators and for those that would like to be counted among them—is that sustaining the advantage from innovation will be found in reaching new levels of process efficiency. For companies that already feel stretched to the limit, Best Innovators offer a fresh perspective.

This chapter is about accelerating innovation profitability by framing processes correctly to begin with and then making sure they remain efficient.

As a group, Best Innovators are distinguished by the coherence of their outlooks—on their markets, on their innovation portfolios, and on the structure of their collaborations inside and outside their organizations. This habit of coherence is rooted in culture and in processes. A predisposition toward strategic coherence among Best Innovators shows up everywhere in the stories they tell us, but it is most evident in their process mindedness.

A look at the corporate histories of Best Innovators reveals again and again that great innovators don't see their processes as discrete. They see them as whole, as components in a machine that generates new products, services, processes, and business models.

Consider Mavi Sud, a small Italian cosmeceutics company that won a Best Innovator award in 2006. Cosmeceutics are therapeutic skin products far removed from conventional cosmetics. For example, Mavi Sud's spray made from chitin, the raw material of a shellfish skeleton, accelerates the healing of burns. Ingenious as its products are, Mavi Sud must compensate for its size disadvantage relative to its multinational competitors, and it does so with unrelenting emphasis on process efficiency. Mavi Sud is in constant direct contact with its client network—dermatologists and pharmacists—to feed its innovation processes. Collaborative supplier relationships feed those processes too, opening the company to the exploration of new search fields such as restorative plastic surgery.

MANAGE COMPLEXITY

Let's be clear: complexity has its virtues. Best Innovators tend to focus less on reducing complexity than on its coherent management. They make a friend of complexity. Managed correctly, complexity creates a real rationale for premium prices and the higher profitability they deliver. For customers, well-managed complexity enhances value with limited adverse impact on a company's costs.

Best Innovators' processes are grounded in a sophisticated understanding of complexity, a perspective that can rewire the way an organization thinks about design, development, and the processes for doing both.

Complexity affects a business across its entire value chain. By definition, complexity touches everything—not just the details of product development but purchasing, internal logistics, production, warehousing, marketing, and freight. Too much complexity or complexity poorly managed can't help but drive up costs.

No matter the industry, the causes of complexity tend to fall into a half dozen broad categories. First of all, there is the intense focus inside most organizations on revenue growth, in which profitability (and the efficiencies that promote it) is too often an afterthought. The preoccupation with revenue growth comes disguised as a virtue, attentive to expanding market share and pleasing customers almost regardless of return.

Some kinds of complexity accumulate over time, almost stealthily. The proliferation of products and their variants, each of which gets its own stock-keeping unit (SKU), sometimes seems to have a logic and momentum all of their own, even though the market might be well-served by fewer and more standardized offerings. This tends to happen because of unclear lines of accountability. Decisions about a product's design and evolution are often made without a comprehensive understanding of interrelated processes and instead spin off eddies of complexity across the value chain.

It is surprising to see how frequently even well-run organizations lack a full understanding of their costs across the value chain. By that, we mean they have a limited grasp of the customization and complexity tradeoffs they are making. They may not even acknowledge these as tradeoffs. Typically, the reasons for this restricted visibility are functional silos that prevent companies from planning for complexity or addressing it when it arises. That makes it hard to understand the nature of complexity and to know what is driving it. When that is the case, how can a company hope to manage complexity all the way through an innovation portfolio?

From our observation of Best Innovators, we've learned to take a holistic approach to both the value of complexity and to its cost. We start by organizing our thinking first about what's *above the skin*—the complexity visible to customers and perceived by customers as value—and then about what's *below the skin*—the cost of complexity they never see.

Examples of above-the-skin value include the number of configurations for a product; the number and interrelationships of a company's marketing divisions, brands, and product lines; and the number of SKUs a company tracks. Examples of below-the-skin costs (often hidden even from an organization's leadership) include the multiple manufacturing processes and technologies a company is managing, the number of product formulations it monitors, and the multiple raw materials it uses across product lines.

When considering the profitability of a product or a service, the questions to answer are developed from identifying which costs can be taken out without sacrificing value above the skin. All along the value chain, every product and service must be questioned for its contribution to revenue, costs, and earnings before interest and tax. The questioning should begin as early as the concept development stage of an innovation portfolio.

Consider the case of a company introducing an innovative new service. The questions this company needs to answer are rather direct: what is the relevance of a market segment for a business unit's revenue? Over the life cycle of the innovation, what is the probable growth in the segment? What is the probability of generating customer loyalty for the new technology? Where is the balance between cost to the company and the value an innovation delivers to customers?

The answers to these questions provide a view into complexity at its most technical levels. At a minimum, they might generate ideas for deleting SKUs that create little value for the customer above the skin and generate only cost below the skin. Better still, they might illuminate new perspectives on the processes underlying the production of a product or service.

LEVERAGE AGILE AND LEAN DESIGN

Complexity, as we've said, has its uses. But it should not accumulate as a consequence of time and inattention. The lean design movement is now about 25 years old. It has its origins in the study of Toyota Motor Corporation's manufacturing methods, which compared with the processes of Western automakers seemed much more focused on customer value and efficient production.[31]

HOW TO BE AGILE

In complex organizations, agility is a function of a long-term view along three dimensions: the *innovation portfolio* (especially with respect to evolving product offerings and customer requirements), the *organizational architecture* and the support it provides (or doesn't provide) to ambitions for its innovation portfolio, and *process planning*.

Among Best Innovators, agility is defined by its emphasis on customer value, committed teams, rapid learning, and openness to change. Here are the basics for developing agility where it may not yet exist:

- Develop and refine ideas incrementally and repeatedly with frequent, time-boxed releases.
- Base development on a prioritized and customer-oriented backlog that translates customer requirements into more refined technical features at each iteration; prioritize high-value activities.
- Empower cross-functional teams with end-to-end responsibility; staff the teams with dedicated individuals who are accountable for the success of the project.
- Reduce feedback time, and deliver frequently with the aim of continuous integration; this is a "test-first" approach characterized by developer regression analysis.
- Validate innovative ideas through active stakeholder participation, inviting successive refinement of requirements.
- Foster a learning-oriented environment by pursuing continuous improvement through the documentation of "lessons learned" and the cultivation of broader competencies in team members.

As a design philosophy, "lean" was noteworthy for two reasons. First, its operational point of view spanned the whole organization, not just manufacturing. Second, its ideal was to make lean design a permanent operational competency, a defined process that started as early as possible in the development of an innovation portfolio.

Management processes are methodologies for compelling conscious behavior. Much of what we admire in the management of Best Innovators are the processes they put in place to heighten organizational awareness of the choices they make in their innovation processes. But we also learn from the ways in which the processes deliver innovation to market—that is to say, in their designs.

Too often, the design process inside an organization is a compartmentalized phenomenon, sequenced among functions. Each piece of the organization adds its perspective (which is good) in isolation from the other pieces (which is bad). Being handed along in sequence from design to production to marketing to service and support will slow even the most innovative idea in its time to profit.

This is a mistake that sounds too obvious to make, and yet in complex organizations, such dysfunction can go unchallenged, even unnoticed. Over a product's life cycle, complexity can accumulate like sedimentary layers of unnecessary cost, to the huge detriment of profitability. A poor design process is often evident only in retrospect.

Take the case of a railcar maker we worked with. Engineers for a passenger car the company was designing specified swing-open windows with locks—even though the car's windows would always be closed to avoid air-flow problems. That was only one instance of what can be called excessive functionality. There were others. For example, there was a dual-battery system for a car that only needed one and flooring that was 40 percent more expensive than what competing railcar makers were using. And a complicated divider-wall design was expensive to install and had pricey separate wall panels. A review of the project determined that because of design waste, each car cost 60 percent more than it needed to cost.

About the only thing missing from the railcar's design was a coherent cross-functional point of view on its core value. That point of view could have delivered a lowest-cost solution that satisfied all customer requirements—the core value—without the many nice-to-haves that added complexity but not much value. Instead, like the story about the blind men designing an elephant, each piece of the organization separately contributed its idea of what the railcar needed. The result was unnecessary functionality, product specs that didn't match the real-world needs of the transportation companies that would operate the car, and interior elements that were out of tune with the company's theoretical commitment to lean manufacturing. No wonder factor costs were high. The hit to profitability was enormous.

Best Innovators have taken lean design to a new level, often called *design to cost*. Think about it like this: the core product functionality of an automobile is its ability to take someone from one place to the next. Creamy leather seats are great, but they are not the car's core function. Getting everyone who touches a product as it travels through an innovation portfolio to think in terms of core functionality is a habit of Best Innovators. At their best, it's more than a habit. It's a process. That's the philosophical heart of lean design, and its logical outcome is design to cost.

HOW BEST INNOVATORS DESIGN TO COST

Function: What does the product or service do, and what should it do?
Specification: How well does the product do what it should do?
Concept: How will what the product must do be accomplished?
Production: How will the product or service be made and delivered?
Factor costs: Where and by whom should the product or service be developed and produced?

Within the design-to-cost frame, collaborators can focus intelligently on a core specification assessment and a core concept assessment. Heightened awareness of these factors created by the design-to-cost approach yields an uncommonly transparent view into core factor costs and a (literal) blueprint to a design for manufacturing.

Our observation of Best Innovators has given us a perspective on lean design that is derived from half a dozen probing questions. It starts with taking an innovation to its theoretical outer limit—in other words, asking the question "Why can't we …?" From there, we work back to a view more constrained by core expectations and core costs: "What must we …?" These two questions frame a cross-functional conversation about core product functionality.

For example, consider a European telecom-equipment maker that used this type of

> *"Platforms play a major role as innovations in themselves and as enablers for 'democratizing' innovations across the organization."*
>
> Ulrich Hackenberg
> CTO
> Volkswagen

cross-functional design methodology to develop a new product. A core-function analysis eliminated an unnecessary circuit breaker and headed off the development of two configurations for a product that only needed one. A redundant direct-current input was eliminated, as was an unused bus port. Subsequently, a core-specification analysis yielded a thinner cable and a simpler connection than what had been called for initially. A core factor-cost analysis prompted the company to solicit new quotes from a lower-cost foreign supplier. In all, the manufacturer saved nearly 65 percent of the originally estimated cost.

In hindsight, a company may see how a clearer indication of where an idea was headed might have yielded a different design that could have gotten it where it wanted to go faster (with less complexity and less cost). But it's never too late. Even well into an innovation's life cycle, it makes sense to take what we sometimes describe as a to-the-bone approach to process management. This entails looking at existing products and processes to see where lean thinking can still be applied all along the value chain, eliminating anything that doesn't add value for the customer.

This is, in effect, like dismantling a product or service to see how it's made—reverse benchmarking, if you will. Could the product be built differently and not just more cheaply? Could the service be delivered with fewer potential barriers between a company and its customers? The yield from this kind of benchmarking can be aggregated and made visible to the organization, encouraging the coherence that gives a complete view of cost and complexity.

THE USEFULNESS OF PLATFORMS

In process terms, benchmarking and design to cost are prerequisites to building platforms—such as the automobile industry's practice of modularization, which promotes interoperability among products and services as well as their multiple generations—all while allowing innovation to take place in separate modules.

Platforms reduce R&D costs and time to market. They permit exceptional flexibility in responding to customer demands, offering on one hand variations defined by any possible combinations of modules and, on the other hand, customized solutions by adapting a single module—all at a lower cost thanks to reduced complexity costs.

In 2005, for instance, the German company Sartorius won a Best Innovator award largely in recognition of its success at reducing time to profit with modularization and redesign. The lab-equipment manufacturer competes around the world and feels acute pressure to accelerate profitability, particularly in mechatronics, its weight and measurement unit. Establishing a standardized product development process, and the consequent use of modular components, reduces development time and cost while increasing the potential for customizing product variants. The Best Innovator judges say the Sartorius approach is a "systematic optimization of the overall value chain by focused optimization projects." It produced an estimated reduction in time to profit of about 15 months.

Volkswagen also excels at building platforms. When the company won its Best Innovator award in 2008, the judges took special note of the ways modular processes that support the company's innovation strategy had taken root across the organization, particularly among business unit heads. They pointed, for example, to the company's platform and modular strategy. Begun more than 15 years ago, that strategy has been the source of countless "toolkits" for the company's engineers, designers, and marketers—all while reducing time to market for innovations.

Most recently, Volkswagen introduced its Modular Transverse Matrix (or Modularer Querbaukasten in German—MQB for short). The platform is now the technical foundation for a large number of cars sharing a uniform engine-mounting position. Modular toolkits cover the entire production process—or as Volkswagen puts it, "from press shop to assembly." They create common standards for the company's factories around the world. Among the benefits of these shared processes is an uncommon flexibility in terms of car models and production runs, including localization of individual car designs. [32]

The Modular Transverse Matrix underlies the designs of cars as different as the Passat and the Audi A4. According to Volkswagen, the platform has reduced the number of engine and transmission variations in these cars by 90 percent. Because gasoline and diesel engines are mounted at exactly the same angle in cars built on the transverse matrix, their exhaust lines, drive shafts, and transmission locations can be standardized. The transverse matrix also enables an identical mounting position for all the company's alternative-drive innovations, from natural gas and hybrids to pure electric drives. Theoretically, all of these models can be produced on the same assembly line, even with different wheelbases and track widths.

In large, complex organizations, platforms such as Volkswagen's Modular Transverse Matrix can create genuine synergies—a better view into complexity, cost-efficient design, and a perspective on innovation that spans the organization. The ideal platform

"In any kind of service industry today, communications and IT will change the business models."

Barbara Dalibard
Managing Director
SNCF Voyages

> *"It's crucial that processes be run on the basis of the best available knowledge."*
>
> Klaus Engel
> CEO
> Evonik

enables technical advancements to be adapted quickly in more than one product line and more than one market segment.

"Platforms play a major role as innovations in themselves and as enablers for 'democratizing' innovations across the organization," says Volkswagen CTO Ulrich Hackenberg. "They help make innovation affordable. They underline our commitment to 'democratizing' innovation." Just a few of the innovations made possible by the transverse matrix in the past few years are lower vehicle weights, improved fuel consumption, and a brake system that reduces post-collision impacts.

Platform building can create a virtuous sequence of savings, reinvestment, and innovation. Volkswagen's production platforms, for example, have led to higher average revenues per car, lower material costs per car, and lower engineered hours per car. These have supported investment in new technologies, making innovations available to high-volume car segments that used to be exclusive to Volkswagen's high-end vehicles. For example, a newly developed family of gasoline engines offers lower weight, lower direct material costs, and higher fuel economy.

Modular approaches "standardize processes in both the direct and the indirect areas of the car group and reduce throughput times in production," Hackenberg says. "They're playing a major role in ensuring that we reach profitability targets."

The utility of a platform, of course, is only as good as the collaborators that use it. Any discussion of processes to maximize the profitability of innovation is hollow without describing the right way to collaborate on processes, whether that collaboration takes place across functions inside the organization or with an array of external partners.

FURTHER IMPROVE CROSS-FUNCTIONAL AND COLLABORATIVE PARTNERSHIPS

Design should be a collaborative, cross-functional process. For example, as the French rail service SNCF explores the development of a door-to-door train service, it is assuming the necessary integration of internal functions, beginning with information technologies.

"In any kind of service industry today," says SNCF's Barbara Dalibard, "communications and IT will change the business models." For example, she envisions using the same tracking technologies that rail lines use for managing freight over long distances to integrate one mode of passenger transport with another.[33]

The reward of a cross-functional process is coherence and a clear understanding of where profitability comes from. The transparency created by using a cross-functional approach to manage innovation processes opens up the organization to, say, a harmonized perspective on specifications or a previously unseen potential for volume bundling. It is a total outlook on the strategic value of an entire product portfolio.

Cross-functional knowledge sharing is a preoccupation we've observed among Best Innovators almost since the competition's beginning in 2003. Integrating all the sources of organizational knowledge, for example, is at the core of Evonik Industries' Idea-to-Profit (I2P) process. I2P tracks data from Evonik's innovation search fields and its competency portfolio. This information flows into a database that steers the innovation process through its entire lifespan, turning ideas and inquiries into new products and services ready for launch or new processes ready for rollout. The cross-functional data stream of I2P informs the tools for forced rankings and portfolio analyses that manage Evonik's exceptionally complex project portfolio of specialty chemicals. Additional features such as system-generated project reports reduce paperwork and improve the efficiency of the innovation-management process, and ultimately profitability.

"It's crucial that processes be run on the basis of the best available knowledge," says Evonik CEO Klaus Engel. "We've formed global teams with interdisciplinary backgrounds to act as data owners. They make sure the project pipeline remains full and that corporate targets—as well as the strategies of the business units and the company as a whole—are taken into consideration."

The rewards of Evonik's pursuit of coherence are projects completed on time and a heightened efficiency for its research activities. That means faster time to market. In just the past few years, projects derived from I2P have added premium-priced specialty materials in fields as diverse as lithium-ion batteries, printable electronics, and the chemistry underlying personal care products.

The ultimate kind of knowledge sharing may eventually be what we currently call big

> "The more rigid and fixed your processes are, the more counterproductive that can be."
>
> Peer Schatz
> CEO
> QIAGEN

data. The phenomenon is among the vogue terms of the moment, and why not? The potential for making sense of unstructured information captured from an array of sources is enormous. There has never been anything like that before.

It has been estimated that 90 percent of all the digital information in existence has been generated in the past two years. There are a number of reasons for this explosion, beginning with the volume of data being captured by compliance policies, sensor-enabled products, and a vast, deep sea of unstructured content. Search engines are providing greater access to unstructured data, including social media. Industry verticals are becoming relentlessly more sophisticated in generating large amounts of data about online behavior, loyalty, point-of-sale activity, and telematics. Developments in analytics include algorithms that can make sense of large volumes of rapidly changing data and even extract predictive elements. As data volume and data complexity explode, traditional processing tools are being eclipsed.

Companies create almost unknowable amounts of information as a byproduct of their products and services. A manufacturer, for instance, has pressure and temperature sensors, batch information on run times and yields, quality-check results, cloud-connected "smart" products, and supply-chain data. If these kinds of data could be connected with more rigor, what effect would that have on improving process efficiency and innovation profitability?

Coca-Cola hopes to answer this question with transaction data collected from its Freestyle vending machines, which transmit information about every interaction with customers. The hope is that capturing real-time data about the choices customers make will translate into very local profiles of a market's taste, perhaps inspiring the formulation of new soft drinks specific to regional bottlers.

Capitalizing on the potential for big data will depend on the same foundational qualities of an innovative culture that we described in the chapter on culture and processes, "Build the Foundation for Innovation and Execution." Knowledge exchange and interconnected networks of talent are essential. These need to be augmented by a deep perspective on privacy law and farsighted security policies. That is especially the case in collaborations with external partners.

THE STRATEGIC VALUE OF COLLABORATIVE PARTNERSHIPS

"The more rigid and fixed your processes are," says Peer Schatz, QIAGEN's CEO, "the more counterproductive that can be. In the past 20 or 25 years that I've had to deal with them, we've again and again questioned them, improved them, or possibly recreated them." In this one respect alone, external partnerships can reframe a company's perspective on its own processes. To put it another way, they can shake things up—or even, in Schatz's term, start anew.

We have discussed the contributions strategic suppliers can make to an innovator's profitability. Collaborative cost reduction is obviously one of them. That comes from offering suppliers meaningful incentives to invest in a company's innovation efforts. But Best Innovators don't just use suppliers to drive out cost. Good suppliers are also partners in idea generation, and they can be essential partners in an implementation process. More than one Best Innovator can tell a story about leveraging its supplier base to be more efficient and to go to market faster.

Managed correctly—by which we mean actively—the external partners in an incumbent's value chains become virtual innovation networks. They can also offer relentless tracking of their own inputs to assure that jointly developed ideas are driven quickly to implementation.

Not long ago, for instance, we worked with an automotive original equipment manufacturer that ran two dozen supplier workshops in one month. It was a classic instance of crowdsourcing by an incumbent innovator. In that month, the company did a design-to-cost appraisal of roughly $670 million in material spending with its suppliers. In that same time, 434 incremental ideas were sketched, and $43 million in potential savings were identified.

As Jon Lindekugel, senior vice president of 3M business development, observes of his company's intimate collaborations with the external partners in which it takes investment stakes, "New venturing does not replace or diminish our internal investment in R&D. We augment our internal development efforts with new venture investments—enabling us to access technology that is one or two adjacencies from our core technology portfolio."

With respect to efficiency and profitability, the greatest contribution an external partner such as a supplier can make is to add a competency that an incumbent does not yet own. This is never more true than when an incumbent is playing catch-up, whether in a new business segment or in relation to a new technology.

Georg Kapsch, CEO of Kapsch Traffic-Com, frames the question as a buy or rent decision. "Short time to market is critical to beating

> *"New venturing does not replace or diminish our internal investment in R&D. We augment our internal development efforts with new venture investments—enabling us to access technology that is one or two adjacencies from our core technology portfolio."*
>
> Jon Lindekugel
> SVP, business development
> 3M

competitors and is achieved by a lean organization and by the partial outsourcing of components or subsystems," he says. "We keep in-house only the core know-how in terms of technology. We outsource what is state of the art."

A good example of what might be a state-of-the-art competency in which incumbents might be playing catch-up is additive manufacturing (AM). A technology with roots in the 1980s, AM builds solid objects from digital images; for that reason, it is frequently called 3D printing. AM's most obvious distinction from traditional manufacturing methods is that instead of cutting or drilling materials, it builds an object a layer at a time—hence "additive."

As a manufacturing innovation, AM has exploded in the past few years. The most common use is for developing prototypes. More and more, it will be used for limited product runs and mass customization. Dentists are already using AM to make crowns and bridges. Airplane makers use it to make parts such as air ducts for advanced fighter jets. Mobile phone manufacturers use AM to print circuits directly onto headsets. BMW, meanwhile, uses printed tools as temporary stand-ins for broken metal tools with long lead times, such as jigs and fixtures. With these AM-aided innovations come unit cost improvements, increased flexibility, and reduced time to market.

Additive manufacturing has its limitations and its skeptics.[34] To make the most of what it can contribute, companies with an AM capability are marrying the technology to conventional manufacturing methods—making it a perfect metaphor for the collaboration between innovative incumbents and external partners.

There are no process panaceas, of course, even in the healthiest collaborative partnerships. Partnerships with external partners can be hard to scale, they complicate intellectual property ownership, and the available partnership models are sometimes much too fluid for comfort. Even acknowledging those hurdles, the reframing and refreshing of processes that strategic partnerships contribute can spike the profitability of new products and sustain an innovative culture for the long haul.

With their habit of thinking about the entire product or service life cycle, Best Innovators reinforce process coherence. This sustains their innovation advantage by amplifying their efficiency—and their profitability.

Best Innovators do not view complexity as an obstacle to efficiency. They make a friend of complexity, creating a context for legitimately higher prices owed to the additional value created for customers. "Value for customers" yields a natural emphasis on core functionality in thinking about product and service design. This design-to-cost approach yields a clear view of core factor costs while spotlighting designed-in waste.

The organizational effect of design to cost is heightened attention to the many choices involved in any innovation processes. These choices are made better with a cross-functional point of view about an innovation portfolio and its core value—that is to say, with a coherent organizational outlook on where profitability comes from. This expansive and, perhaps paradoxically, *focused* view of collaboration is evident in relationships with strategic suppliers, with which Best Innovators partner to drive out costs, hatch new ideas, and develop implementation processes.

The cumulative effect of this intense attention to efficiency—the coherence in this approach to the innovation portfolios—is faster time to market, accelerated time to profit, and sustained profitability.

INNOVATION LEADER AMAZON RELIES ON TEAM EFFORT

In 1997, three years after Amazon's launch, founder Jeff Bezos told *Inc.* magazine, "There's nothing about our model that can't be copied over time."[35] But even then, Amazon was playing a long game. Bezos made that clear to investors in the company's first prospectus, which said bluntly, "The company's view ... is that it will incur substantial losses for the foreseeable future."

Bezos wasn't joking. Amazon did not report its first profitable year until 2001, seven years after launching. But unlike so many other hot names from the late 1990s, Amazon survived the bursting of the dot-com bubble and continues to grow.

Starting life as an online bookseller, Amazon has become known as "the everything store," selling just about anything you can put in a box and ship, from electronics and fine art to clothing and groceries. From its beginnings, Amazon's innovation strategy has been business-model innovation, application imagination, and a fresh perspective on and transformation of seemingly settled business practices and technologies. Amazon saw what was right in front of everyone else, and it moved first. The result was a new experience for consumers.

Bezos was right when he said rivals would copy its innovations. After being introduced by Amazon, above-the-skin innovations such as 1-Click and Recommendations and below-the-skin innovations such as fulfillment processing and digital publishing became mainstream phenomena. Amazon has persistently moved into businesses not ordinarily associated with online retailing, most notably with its 2007 introduction of the Kindle, which made reading digital books commonplace. Its web services unit, launched in 2006 to make use of Amazon's excess information technology infrastructure, is now a

$4 billion business.

In late 2013, Bezos paid $250 million for *The Washington Post*. If ever there was an industry in need of business-model innovation, it is newspapering, which has been struggling to find its way forward for nearly 20 years.

"In my experience," said Bezos at the time of *The Post*'s acquisition, "the way invention, innovation, and change happen is (through) team effort. There's no lone genius who figures it all out and sends down the magic formula. You study, you debate, you brainstorm, and the answers start to emerge. It takes time."[36]

AGGRESSIVE, OPEN INNOVATION A HABIT AT EVONIK

One of the world's leading specialty-chemicals companies, Evonik operates in an arena with many of the same competitive dynamics as commodities and raw-materials businesses. The difference is that Evonik has to understand the total value chain for multiple industries, from automobiles and construction to pharmaceuticals and beyond. Evonik wants to be a preferred supplier to all of these companies and knows that being an aggressive innovator is the path to get there.

Since its spinout from the RAG mining group in 2007, Evonik has grown to be a €13.629 billion company. From its beginnings, the German company consciously laid the foundation for a culture of innovation. Internally, for example, it bestows an annual innovation award for outstanding application-oriented research. It is an active practitioner of using search fields to frame its innovation strategy. These search fields are mapped against growth targets and against the company's competency portfolios. These include particle design, coating and bonding sciences, interfacial technologies, polymer design, biotechnology, and catalytic processes.

Evonik has also established a strategic innovation unit, Creavis, to oversee medium- to long-term innovation projects, including the creation of what the company calls competence platforms. Within what are called project houses, Creavis manages cross-functional collaborations among Evonik business units. Talented individuals from the business units are loaned to a project house for as long as three years before returning to their regular jobs, bringing back with them new knowledge and a widened perspective. Currently, Evonik is running two project houses: a light-and-electronics project in Taiwan and a composites initiative in Marl, about 40 kilometers north of Evonik's headquarters in Essen, Germany.

It is in the nature of the specialty-chemicals business that cross-functional collaboration becomes an operational habit. Accelerating speed to market is an essential KPI for these collaborative teams, as it is for Evonik's multiple external partnerships.

"Open innovation is the next step in innovation management for the specialty-chemicals industry," says CEO Klaus Engel. "Real innovation takes place beyond the borders separating companies and industries."

VOLKSWAGEN STRIVES TO BE WORLD'S MOST INNOVATIVE

The Volkswagen Group, headquartered in Wolfsburg, Germany, is the leading carmaker in Europe and among the largest in the world. Every year, 13 percent of all passenger cars sold around the world are made by Volkswagen. In 2012, the company's worldwide revenue totaled €193 billion. A company this large has a special challenge in sustaining competitive dynamism.

When Volkswagen won the overall Best Innovator award in 2008, the judges noted that responsibility for innovation is deeply rooted in senior management's vision. The senior team names a tangible set of deliverables from the company's innovation strategy: it has a goal of increasing unit sales to more than 10 million vehicles a year. It intends to do that while sustaining a return on sales before tax of at least 8 percent. Such ambitions are intended to assure a solid financial position. But just as important, it will preserve Volkswagen's freedom to act even in difficult economic periods.

Volkswagen has given itself the advantage of a plainly defined target: it aims to position itself as the world's most innovative high-volume brand. And it has set a stretch goal for 2018: it wants to be the world's leading automaker in terms of value and environmental responsibility.

SNCF VOYAGES COMMITTED TO INNOVATION CULTURE

When a French jury awarded SNCF Voyages the Best Innovator service prize in 2013, it took note of what it called "a clear strategic vision" built on four pillars: employees, customers, profitable growth, and operational performance. What caught the jury's eye was how well-integrated these pillars were in the generation of ideas through structured approaches, including price setting.

SNCF Voyages is one of the five divisions of France's national railway, SNCF. Among the unit's services are high-speed passenger rail in France, including TGV (train à grande vitesse, or high-speed train) and Ouigo, a low-fare service. Within France, Voyages also provides Eurostar, Thalys, TGV Lyria, TGV Italia, Italo, Westbahn, and a Deutsche Bahn and SNCF partnership. In addition to being France's leading online travel agency, SNCF Voyages operates a growing long-distance coach company, iDBUS, launched in July 2012.

In 2012, SNCF Voyages generated revenue of €7.5 billion, 20 percent of which came from international operations.

SNCF Voyages has ambitions for building an innovation culture that—unfairly—one might not associate with state-owned enterprises. Competition, as CEO Barbara Dalibard points out, "comes from everywhere and crosses historical boundaries. Videoconferences compete with travel. That forces us to rethink our business from transportation to mobility."

When she speaks of the difference between transportation and mobility, she is speaking not of travel from one station to another but from one's home to a final destination. The goal SNCF has set is to create a way for passengers to combine and personalize the company's many travel offerings. Re-imagining its business model in this way, Dalibard argues, can make SNCF Voyages the first choice for passengers as Europe opens to competition from other rail companies.

A good example of the unit's commitment to innovation is its new business model for train travel, Ouigo, which connects the Paris region and southeastern France. Launched in February 2013, Ouigo is a low-cost, high-speed train: €10 for adults and €5 for children. Dalibard boasts that Ouigo was built by her entire organization, from train crews and ticket agents to marketing and strategy teams.

"We have solid foundations for innovation," she says, especially on the cultural dimension—a culture that she says has roots in SNCF's origins as an engineering company. The company is also consciously strengthening its innovation portfolio and taking aim at accelerating its time to market. Progress is still to be made, Dalibard acknowledges, on innovation profitability.

With those goals in mind, the company collaborates with strategic suppliers. These partnerships are varied, from rethinking the food served aboard TGV trains and reinventing the ticketing process to working with universities to build flow-management models that use big-data techniques for booking and traveling.

"What we sell is an everyday consumer product," Dalibard says. "Innovation is a strong enabler in differentiating ourselves and convincing very diverse populations with different purchasing powers and different needs to take the train."

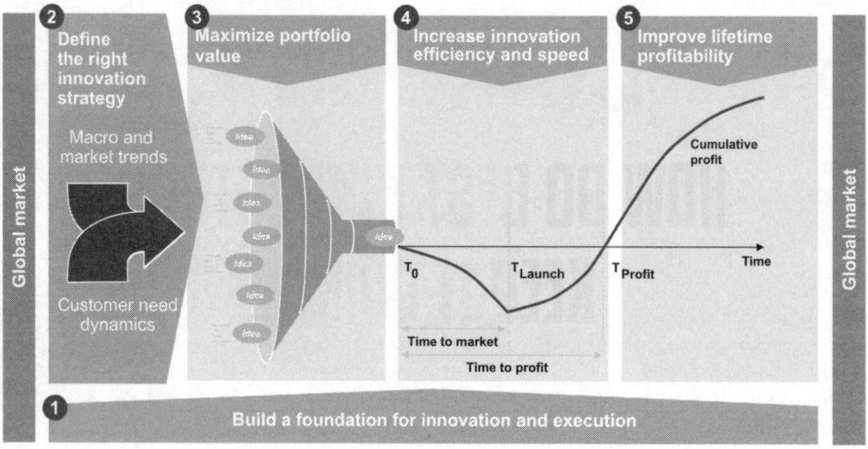
Global market
2 Define the right innovation strategy
Macro and market trends
Customer need dynamics
3 Maximize portfolio value
4 Increase innovation efficiency and speed
5 Improve lifetime profitability
Cumulative profit
T0
TLaunch
TProfit
Time
Time to market
Time to profit
Global market
1 Build a foundation for innovation and execution

CHAPTER 7

HOW DO BEST INNOVATORS KEEP IT GOING?

A nyone who expects sustained, significant growth will never get it by doing what they are already doing, only better. Substantial growth comes from delivering on durable innovation strategies, durable in their constancy and durable in their structured openness to change. This is, once again, a tension—one Best Innovators manage well because they take great care in building their leadership teams.

In nearly all of our conversations with Best Innovators since 2003, most members of the senior management team sooner or later mention their preoccupation with sustaining creative momentum. Ask Tata Motors' former vice chairman Ravi Kant about his concerns, and he answers point blank, "The main challenge for Tata Motors will be to maintain its leading position."

Kant's bluntness makes sense. We operate in an era when historical growth rates cannot be expected (certainly not for incumbents) and when volatility is the norm on every dimension that matters. Evonik CEO Klaus Engel could be speaking for all incumbents when he says, "The global environment will be dramatically altered by the challenges of resource scarcity, climate change, urbanization, a growing world population, and the shift of industrial production to China, India, Brazil, and other emerging economies."

Volkswagen CTO Ulrich Hackenberg makes much the same point. "We are faced with an increasingly global market, with all that implies about new customers and different needs," he says. "But let's not forget there are opportunities as well. Connectivity, social media, and so on create engineering challenges. But they also open up new ways to communicate with customers and for us to provide new services and solutions."

Best Innovators are built to withstand uncertainty. Unrelenting focus on their innovation programs—measurable in their KPIs—is what has enabled them to ride out market shocks in the past. That same quality will sustain them in the future, which can be counted on to have at least its fair share of shocks.

To start with, they will need the kind of leadership that is neither easily found nor easily defined. In our final chapter we highlight some characteristics of Best Innovators and why they outperform their peers (see figure 9):

- **Lead by example.** Create flat organizations guided by senior teams. What senior managers think, say, and do makes all the difference between an innovation culture that lasts and one that doesn't.

- **Be constant, be comprehensive.** Continually improve innovation performance by addressing all value levers described in the previous chapters simultaneously. Of course, the focus may change over time, but in the long run, the result is a balanced orchestration of all five value levers.

- **Communicate strategy with clarity.** Create a common language of innovation—an easily grasped expression of this statement: "We are doing *these* things for *these* reasons." This creates alignment in and out of the organization.

Figure 9

Best Innovators outperform the competition

Long-term performance of automotive OEMs
(Industry comparison vs. Best Innovators, 2003 to 2013[1])

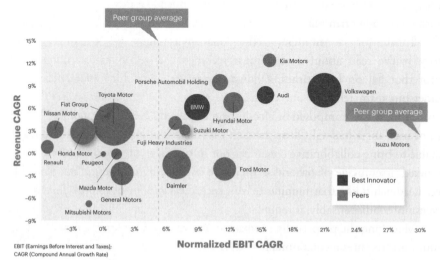

EBIT (Earnings Before Interest and Taxes);
CAGR (Compound Annual Growth Rate)

[1] Peer companies selected from Forbes Global 2000 ranking, not including those from fast-moving emerging markets (primarily China and India)
Sources: Forbes, Thomson Reuters Datastream; A.T. Kearney analysis

---

- **Manage with an expectation of volatility.** Acknowledge that it is a turbulent world and pay attention to movements in operating environments, draw conclusions, and act on them.

LEAD BY EXAMPLE

In every chapter, we have described the flatness of Best Innovator organizations. It is a flatness manifest in the many ways in which work and decision making are distributed among teams that cross functions and that in many cases cross the structural boundaries of the organization.

Don't make the mistake of thinking Best Innovators are organic collaborators that manage themselves. Best Innovators are guided by senior teams. What those teams think and *do* makes all the difference between an innovation culture that lasts and one that doesn't.

Georg Kapsch observes that for senior managers, "the main innovation challenges are keeping up the culture, not getting satisfied in times of good results, and getting the right people with the right mindset. If we're going to be permanently innovative, we're going to be looking beyond the borders of our business and trying to rethink our whole industry day by day. Otherwise, sooner or later, as a company, we'll fall behind."

If we know one thing about senior executives like Kapsch, it is that innovation for them is not an initiative. They are committed to their innovation strategies as permanent features of their organizational cultures. Building the culture is a long-term play.

Think for a moment about some story you've read about a once-great innovator that fell on hard times. Odds are the leadership team fell into one of two categories. Either it was composed of a collection of "mini-me's" of a bad CEO, or the CEO was unable to bring collaborative coherence out of a mixed assemblage of otherwise smart people. Leadership like that requires intelligence. Even more indispensably, it requires trust.

Managing the perpetually innovative organization requires a conglomerate leadership style—or perhaps we should say a conglomerate kind of leadership team. Ideally, senior

> *"The main innovation challenges are keeping up the culture, not getting satisfied in times of good results, and getting the right people with the right mindset."*
>
> Georg Kapsch
> CEO
> Kapsch TrafficCom

managers will have a taste for experimenting and exploring and will transmit that taste to the organization, mainly by their behavior. But organizations also need process discipline to realize the commercial potential of their ideas and product innovations. An idea is not an innovation until customers are buying it. Someone has to manage that evolution—and manage it actively.

The ideal senior manager can simultaneously spark creativity and maintain process discipline. Creativity and process discipline are not opposites, even if they are often portrayed as such. Managers don't need to choose between them. Within Best Innovators, senior leaders accept risk as a companion to real innovation, but they do so while helping their organizations understand the definition of acceptable risk. Leaders like that have the fortitude to stick with a project with a long-term payoff while still knowing how to kill a project once it becomes obvious that even a good idea won't be commercially viable—all while extracting useful lessons from the experience.

There's a balance to be struck, obviously, between a leader with a strong directive style and one who works for consensus. Good managers cultivate that balance within themselves. But human nature being what it is, senior leaders often lean in one direction. That's why leadership teams need to be intentionally assembled collaborations of an array of personalities.[37]

Here's an interesting side note: although we can all find examples to the contrary, striking the right balance in a senior leader appears to come more readily when candidates for leadership jobs already have a presence inside the organization. A study of non-financial companies in the S&P 500 by A.T. Kearney and the Kelley School of Business at Indiana University showed that in the 20 years between 1988 and 2007, organizations that exclusively promoted CEOs from within their own ranks outperformed companies that recruited from outside. The 36 companies that exclusively promoted from within outperformed their peers on multiple metrics: return on assets, equity and investment, revenue and earnings growth, earnings per share growth, and stock-price appreciation.

This Homegrown CEO study concluded that boards of directors too often do a poor job of succession planning.[38] Instead of focusing on developing leaders and building a stable of internal candidates, boards too often go outside their organization in search of a star. And more often than not, shareholders pay the price right from the beginning of the new executive's tenure: compensation for an externally sourced CEO is, on average, 65 percent higher than it would have been for a homegrown candidate.

Over the long term, no non-financial member of the S&P 500 that recruited its CEO externally generated 20-year performance numbers that surpassed or even equaled those of the top 36 companies in the study. Imagine the consequences of choosing the wrong leader for Best Innovators, which build their cultures to last far longer than 20 years. For Best Innovators, a poor fit in a senior leadership job has a much greater consequence than an oversized compensation package.

The Homegrown CEO study speaks volumes about the power of an innovation culture. It will always be hard to find a star for senior leadership roles, no matter how they are recruited. But finding stars is the wrong focus for organizational development. We say this well aware that many of the often-told stories about great innovators feature a single dynamic character at the heart of the plot. What matters is the totality of the organizational culture. What matters is coherent commitment to process. What matters is the selection of the senior team.

BE CONSTANT, BE COMPREHENSIVE

Tata Motors' former vice chairman Ravi Kant knows the automaker will have to improve upon its current capabilities and build new ones if it wants to extend the success of the past 15 years. He ticks off several areas where he would like to see the company be strong: scenario planning, predictive analysis using big data, rich competitive intelligence, and greater closeness to Tata's customers. That's a strong list of to-do's, and looking at Tata's record of innovation since the introduction of the Ace light truck, no one can argue with the company's ambition. How will innovators such as Tata sustain momentum and continue to deliver?

First, they will be constant in their comprehensive approach to the five value levers of a permanently innovative company—in other words, they will be coherent in managing the processes described in this book. Being deep in one or two of the levers will never be enough to sustain Best Innovators over the long run. It takes the balanced orchestration of all five.

Best Innovators are serious about innovation culture, and it shows in the behavior of their senior teams. If, as we've argued, culture is the sum of what is prized by an organization, then the first job of leadership in the perpetually innovative organization is to actively work at creating a culture where smart people are not merely permitted but enabled to thrive.

"To have a company that can execute but which is at the same time very flexible—that will be the great challenge," says Enrico Zito, CEO of Whirlpool Brazil's appliance unit.

Some of the things senior managers do to create this culture and sustain their innovation machines might seem obvious. They nourish, for example, col-

> *"To have a company that can execute but which is at the same time very flexible—that will be the great challenge."*
>
> Enrico Zito
> CEO, appliance unit
> Whirlpool Brazil

legiality in all parts of the organization so that strong minds have a structured way of being commercially creative. As we've pointed out, necessary as they are, the independence and entrepreneurialism synonymous with collegiality carry risk. A noble failure should not be a threat to anyone's career, but the risk of failure must still be managed. The starting place for this kind of risk management is a well-described account of the strategic meaning of innovation for the organization. That account gives structure to everyone's thinking about where a new idea might one day go. Communicating it clearly is among the responsibilities of an innovator's leadership team.

Leaders of Best Innovators can describe explicit expectations for their innovation strategy—its contribution to growth, the segments in which their companies will compete, the capabilities their organizations will need to win, and the deliverables to which they commit their organizations. To the extent that these are made explicit, they can't help but be reflected in the processes they devise.

By now, it should be clear that an essential condition of innovation is collaboration across functions and across geographies. Such collaborations are complex and require the support of coherent process management. Best Innovators see their processes as part of a whole, as components of the permanently innovative company. The coherence of their view comes from a focus on core functionality, which is to say from the attention paid to the central job a product or service delivers to customers.

If, for example, the progressive phases of an innovation portfolio are part of a stage-gate process—and they are—then the stage-gating process is a direct manifestation of all the elements the senior team has put into defining the innovation strategy. Not the least of these elements is the senior team's thinking about where the organization will be in the future.

Leaders of Best Innovators treat farsightedness as an organizational capability. We hear this all the time in our conversations with senior teams. It explains their preoccupation, for example, with transfer rates—the measure of how many good ideas actually make it out of the innovation portfolio and into the market. But leaders of Best Innovators are practical people. For them, the decisive KPI will always be reduced time to profit, the measure of how long it takes an idea to begin earning back the investment made in it and to lay claim to the title "innovation."

The practicality reflected in this outlook is the precondition for the collaborative spirit. Practicality is probably the most pronounced characteristic of Best Innovator management teams. Practicality is the reason they so readily pursue what we've called interoperability—the readiness to share knowledge, budget, time, and talent wherever they are needed in support of innovation strategy. Practicality informs their active collaborations with external partners, especially suppliers. They know that strategic external partners can fill capability gaps, shorten time to market, elevate functionality, and reduce costs. "A company can have a strong tech portfolio, but it only creates value when we connect it to the needs of customers and markets," says 3M's head of R&D, Ashish Khandpur.

But what is the right leadership style for accomplishing things while building out a perpetually innovative culture? And where do those leaders come from?

COMMUNICATE STRATEGY WITH CLARITY

Among the things leaders of all Best Innovators have in common is, probably first of all, an ability to communicate the vision behind their innovation strategy. Without the shared language of a common vision, there can be no alignment, no galvanizing idea that makes itself felt right across the company and even out to the company's constellation of partners and collaborators.

Someone once said that a clear idea is one that can be written on the back of a business card. An innovation strategy may need to be a little more elaborate than that, but for the purposes of communicating strategy in a way that excites an organization, the expression of the strategic vision should be no more than a page. The logistics needed to make the vision happen require a deeper level of detail, of course, but the rationale behind an innovation strategy should be an easily grasped expression of this statement: "We are doing *these* things for *these* reasons."

An essential talent in a senior manager is the ability to plainly define an innovation strategy (and the strategic reasoning supporting it). Too often, we see the job of defining

> *"We are faced with an increasingly global market with all that implies about new customers and different needs. But let's not forget there are opportunities as well."*
>
> Ulrich Hackenberg
> CTO
> Volkswagen

innovation strategy relegated to the communications function, feeling as it does like one of those soft skills that can't be measured for its operational impact and is therefore not considered rigorous. If a function is not considered rigorous, then it is a secondary concern to an operational management team. This is wrong. Like so many soft skills, an ability to express an idea clearly is a difference-maker for senior leaders in creating alignment, building an enduring innovation culture, and explaining the logic of processes to talented people in and out of an organization.

British novelist E.M. Forster once remarked, "How do I know what I think until I see what I say?" The effort to express the continuing rationale for an innovation strategy pays off first in the clarity it creates for the senior team by compelling it to name its priorities—in other words for the team members to explain their innovation strategy to themselves first of all. This cannot help but create transparency defining core and non-core activities. And that, as described in the chapter "Define the Right Innovation Strategy," is the beginning of the logic chain that defines the architecture of the innovation portfolio. It starts all the way back at the search fields in which a company's value-chain network will be active. This is true whether the term "network" refers to cross-functional internal teams or to external partners.

In this book, we have devoted a good deal of attention to collaboration with strategic suppliers. Best Innovators do a good job of managing the pitfalls of external relationships. Success in this area derives from the hard work Best Innovators do in defining a common understanding of their innovation goals to their audience, whether that audience is in or out of their organizations. They adopt what might be called a unified language of innovation to clarify communication between themselves and their suppliers. This aligns suppliers' goals with their own. In practical terms, a unified language for talking about innovation strategy underpins agreement on legal issues, such as the ownership of intellectual property. It is indispensable for reaching consensus on time and quality management.

For example, Rational AG, the German manufacturer of combi steamers for commercial kitchens, attributes its success with strategic partnerships to a clear expression of what it needs from external collaborators. A strategic supplier to Rational, for instance, must be an innovator itself. Why? So that it can amplify Rational's existing ideas and inventions, encouraging the company to push even harder into new frontiers. Getting this shared sense of mission right is expressed in reduced time to market, reduced time to profit, and a coherently managed innovation life cycle.

We are not arguing that the expression of innovation strategy needs to be poetic—although come to think of it, why not? A talent for powerful expression can electrify people in their attachment to an idea, and that is no small thing.

MANAGE WITH AN EXPECTATION OF VOLATILITY

In 2012, A.T. Kearney developed its Turbulence Index, which offers a live view of volatility in the world economy by combining five measures of price movements—not prices but their movement. It turns out the sensation of instability isn't your imagination. The world economy really is in a period of exceptional volatility, testing the skills of managers in organizations of all sizes with aspirations to sustained records of innovation (see figure 10).[39]

"Management that is destructively critical when mistakes are made kills initiative. And it's essential that we have many people with initiative if we are to continue to grow."

William L. McKnight
Former President
3M

The picture of extraordinary volatility quantified by the Turbulence Index demonstrates what we all intuitively know about the growing influence of externalities on senior executives and the companies they manage. The fact of volatility and the uncertainty it creates underscores the challenge of taking a long-term view of the world and its absolute necessity.

Even with imperfect knowledge, Best Innovators recognize that sustaining the momentum of their inventiveness—measurable in KPIs such as new-product vitality—relies on owning a point of view about the future. Best Innovators are not simply placing bets on what the future holds. Instead, they are paying attention to movements in their operating environments (as well as outside of them) and drawing their own conclusions.

A LIVE VIEW OF VOLATILITY

A.T. Kearney's Turbulence Index portrays volatility in a basket of externalities, including food, foreign exchange rates, metals, energy, and publicly traded shares. High volatility in those areas is likely to be with us for a long while. Translating that knowledge into choices for specific companies depends on understanding volatility's impact on profit and loss, starting with the planning premises guiding the pacing of innovation portfolios.

The Turbulence Index is a moving average of five international measures of price movements: the U.N. Food and Agriculture Organization's Food Price Index, the European Central Bank's foreign exchange rates, the International Monetary Fund's index of commodity metals prices, the Chicago Board Options Exchange Volatility Index measuring market expectations of near-term volatility in Standard & Poor's 500 stock-index option prices, and the Dow Jones-Union Bank of Switzerland Commodity Index sub-index of energy prices for crude oil, heating oil, natural gas, and unleaded gasoline. Each element is equally weighted with a 20 percent value. Each is a variable, and these variables interact.

The picture of extraordinary volatility painted by the Turbulence Index quantifies what we all sense about the growing influence of externalities on senior executives and the companies they manage. It illustrates macroeconomic uncertainty, financial instability, and unprecedented thirst for resources in an age of unpredictable energy and commodity prices. Energy prices, for example, have an impact on food prices because petrochemicals are essential to fertilizer production. Energy prices also have uneven ef-

Figure 10

The world economy is in an especially volatile period

Global Business Policy Council Volatility Index, 1999-2011
(1999=100)

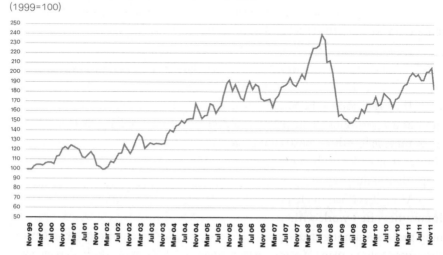

Sources: U.N. Food and Agriculture Organizations, European Central Bank, International Monetary Fund, Chicago Board Options Exchange Volatility Index, Dow Jones-Union Bank of Switzerland Commodity Index; A.T. Kearney analysis

fects on currency exchange rates, depending on a country's reliance on imported oil. These interactions are not always predictable and are often clear only in retrospect.

Looking at the Turbulence Index over time, it is easy to see how volatility is excited by external events that impose themselves on several variables at once. Unpredicted temporal factors—so-called "Black Swans"—such as war and natural catastrophe come into play. Consider, for instance, the 2003 Iraq invasion's impact on oil prices, the 2008 world financial crisis, or the effect of the 2011 Japanese tsunami on worldwide supply chains. The Turbulence Index offers insight into the interdependence of the world's economies.

The impact of turbulence differs by industry. For instance, agribusinesses are subject to the full range of turbulence variables. Automakers are sensitive to particular variables such as the price of steel. A bank has minimal sensitivity to uncertainty because the cost of its principal inputs—labor and real estate—doesn't fluctuate much, even over extended periods.

The Turbulence Index offers a foundation for analytics that, approached with the coherence characteristic of Best Innovators, can guide choices about innovation portfolios, resourcing, and talent management.

Some companies have already learned to capitalize on a holistic view of turbulence. For example, a fast-moving consumer goods company introduced choice into its supply chain by doubling the number of strategic suppliers in Asia. A global food company conducted a portfolio review and methodically trimmed volatile—and, as it happened, asset-intensive—businesses.

Managing turbulence cannot be a one-time, crisis-driven event. Expectations of high volatility must be built into processes by which we manage businesses. The Turbulence Index is a way to do exactly that, beginning with planning processes.

This attention to the future shapes the way Best Innovators populate their innovation portfolios. It shapes the conception of the organizations they build to commercialize those portfolios. Attention to the future informs the tactical choices they make in the near term and guides them in their determination to shape their industries.

As we described in chapter 3 "Define the Right Innovation Strategy," Best Innovators often work with 10-year planning horizons. By comparison, planning processes among their peers are often as short as a year out or perhaps a three-year rolling plan. We might call this near-termism. It leads to what our A.T. Kearney colleagues Jochen Kaempfer and Maurice Violani once named "temporal myopia," a condition in which a company can't see industry changes stealthily eroding a currently profitable competitive position.[40]

The moral hazard lurking for short-term thinkers is that, in our demonstrably volatile age, temporal myopia can be mistaken for flexibility and resiliency. Short-term thinkers would not say they are failing to think about the future. They are instead learning by doing and setting strategy from the front lines. What they are missing is the threat this creates to the nurturing of long-term capabilities. Subtly, it encourages incrementalism at the expense of innovation.

For example, beginning with the digital revolution 20 years ago, far too many telecommunications providers used the volatility created by what we were all calling convergence to de-emphasize long-term thinking in favor of short-term moves that slowed the erosion of fixed-line revenue. This was at a time when every telecom in the world knew mobile technologies would slowly kill their core business. The implication was that they would work out a perspective on digital—well, sometime. Now we are living in what would have been considered the long run in the mid-1990s. And how many telecoms can you name that led the way with transformative innovations, took command of the convergence phenomenon, and now dominate the industry?

We could make an identical observation about bricks-and-mortar retailers. Many have done a remarkable job of staying afloat with strategies involving store locations, operations, and merchandising. But every year, retail growth comes more from innovative online alternatives. That has been true for 20 years.

The burden on the managers of Best Innovators is to resist relentless investor pressure for short-term profitability. (Certain Silicon Valley start-ups have been reluctant to talk about profitability to an extreme.) The model might be the online retailing giant, Amazon. Every year in the company's annual report, CEO Jeff Bezos reprints his first letter to shareholders after the company's IPO in 1997, in which he wrote, "We will continue to make investment decisions in light of long-term market leadership considerations rather than short-term profitability considerations or short-term Wall Street reactions." Reprinting the letter is Amazon's not-so-subtle way of reminding investors that the company famous for its retail innovations is still playing a long-term game and that it will continue playing it even in a business that shows no sign of relinquishing the volatility that has characterized it since birth.

"Cells mutate constantly in their effort to improve," observes QIAGEN CEO Peer Schatz. "There's always a risk of negative or no effect, and sometimes diseases arise. But biology is admirable in its compulsion to change. We want to have that same compulsion, that same constant ability to change."

In Schatz's analogy is all of what it means to be a Best Innovator. Being perpetually innovative is not just a reaction to change in the operating environment, or an initiative. It is a way of life.

All organizations talk about growth, especially if they have shareholders who expect to see it every quarter. What is distinctive about Best Innovators is that their conversations about growth don't default to the conventional top-line and bottom-line dichotomy. Their strategic vision is much larger than that. They envision building new businesses again and again, not just managing the ones they already own. Their vision is years out into the future.

It is not at all surprising that leadership teams for Best Innovators stay awake worrying about how they will continue fueling their innovations. That is the culture they have created. All across their organizations but especially among the senior teams, there is a fixation on the evolution of the business. Their futures depend on the right calibration of collegiality, creativity, and process discipline. The ability to manage the inevitable tensions among those three things is near the top on the list of qualifications for a senior manager's role inside a Best Innovator. Not surprisingly, it helps if managers come to their jobs already steeped in the innovation culture with which they've been entrusted.

When talking to the leaders of Best Innovators, we are always struck by how concisely they can talk about the goals for their innovation strategies and about the capabilities they will need to realize these goals. A Best Innovator is a complex, forever-moving thing. Managing it coherently requires a clear vision of a company's direction and a talent for sharing that vision with every member of the organization.

Central to that vision is profitability. Concern for profitability forms the creative process. It defines the stage gates of innovation portfolios and determines the processes by which businesses are managed. It stimulates a fixation on the future and the conclusions that the organization draws about the meaning of that future.

Our future is likely to be volatile. Uncertainty will be the norm. For incumbents especially, growth in a world of uncertainty won't come just from squeezing costs or outsourcing. It will come from unrelenting, rigorous attention to innovation as a way of life in the way Peer describes it.

In the fall of 2014, A.T. Kearney surveyed more than 800 European managers from a broad range of business segments and industry sectors. Respondents expect sales from products and services commercialized over the past three years to bring in a growing share of revenues: 66 percent say these sales will represent more than a quarter of their revenues by 2015, and even more—76 percent—say this will be the case by 2030.

When providing their estimates for 2015, 62 percent attribute more than a quarter of new product or service sales to collaboration with third parties. The importance of collaborative innovation to generate revenues depends little on the size of the business. In the future, collaborative innovation with external partners is expected to take on a bigger role: 71 percent attribute more than a quarter of new product sales to collaboration with third parties when providing their estimates for 2030.

Yet, while collaborative innovation is clearly becoming a key capability, especially with suppliers, there are still significant barriers and difficulties to overcome. For example, A.T. Kearney's 2014 Assessment of Excellence in Procurement study finds that a majority of companies lack the following:

- Internal capacity to leverage suppliers effectively (84%)
- Systems and measures in place to illustrate suppliers' contributions to innovation (83%)
- Internal transparency and understanding needs for future growth (76%)
- Willingness to invest time, resources, or money in developing partnerships with suppliers (72%)

These internal barriers need to be tackled in the near future. For larger companies, doing so will require partially transformative actions in order to maintain a competitive advantage.

Great organizations are built to capitalize on uncertainty. They don't merely adapt to change. They create change, and they own it. The track records of Best Innovators prove it.

ACKNOWLEDGEMENTS

As we stipulated on several occasions throughout these chapters, collaboration both internally and externally is essential to translating ideas into innovations. The same is true for the development of this book, which would not have been possible without the strong support of our A.T. Kearney colleagues and the winners of the Best Innovator competitions.

First and foremost, we wish to thank the Best Innovator companies and senior leaders who shared their thoughtful insights on how innovation, when well-managed, drives profitable growth: Jacques Aschenbroich (Valeo), Jeff Bezos (Amazon), Günter Blaschke (Rational), Gottfried Brunbauer (Rosenbauer), Jean-Marc Chery (STMicroelectronics), Barbara Dalibard (SNCF), Nicholas Davis (WEF), Klaus Engel (Evonik), Roberto Fedeli (Ferrari), Gildeon Filho (Chemtech), Ulrich Hackenberg (Volkswagen), Rolf Hollander (CEWE Color), Manel Jadraque (Desigual), Ravi Kant (Tata), Georg Kapsch (Kapsch), Tomáš Kolář (LINET), Thomas Müller-Kirschbaum (Henkel), Jan Musil (ČKD Group), Tetsuji Ohashi (Komatsu), Bruno Piacenza (Henkel), Abel Rochinha (Coelce), Peer Schatz (QIAGEN), Inge Thulin (3M), Guy Wollaert (Coca-Cola), and Enrico Zito (Whirlpool).

Also, special thanks to the A.T. Kearney partners who supported the Best Innovator competitions over the past years and contributed to this book: Inigo Aranzabal (Madrid), Hanjo Arms (Berlin), Johan Aurik (Brussels), Gotfred Berntsen (Oslo), Werner Borrmann (Düsseldorf), Alex Blanter (San Francisco), Paul Carrannanto (Washington, DC), Claudio Cervellati (Milan), Daniela Chikova (Vienna), Pascal Colombani (Paris), Ulli Dannath (Berlin), Florian Dickgreber (Düsseldorf), Laurent Dumarest (Paris), Lars Eismark (Copenhagen), Torsten Eistert (Frankfurt), Axel Erhard (Munich), Marcus Eul (Düsseldorf), Richard Forrester (London), Axel Freyberg (Berlin), Dario Gaspar (São Paulo), Carsten Gerhardt (Düsseldorf), Jules Goffre (Munich), Wolfgang Haag (Düsseldorf), Mike Hales (Chicago), Martin Handschuh (Stuttgart), David Hanfland (Chicago), Florian Haslauer (Vienna), Hagen Götz Hastenteufel (Berlin), Martin Haubensak (Düsseldorf), Per Hong (Moscow), Joachim von Hoyningen-Huene (Munich), Bo Kaunitz (Stockholm), Masahiro Kishida (Tokyo), Götz Klink (Stuttgart), Jil Krakowski (New York), Robert Kremlicka (Vienna), Fritz Kröger (Berlin), Stephan

Krubasik (Munich), Marc Lakner (Berlin), Volker Lang (Munich), Tobias Lewe (Düsseldorf), Andreas Liedtke (Zürich), Daniel Mahler (New York), Manish Mathur (Gurgaon), Stephan Mayer (Stuttgart), Xavier Mesnard (Paris), Dietrich Neumann (Berlin), Geir Olson (Oslo), Peter Pfeiffer (Düsseldorf), Andreas Pratz (Munich), Thomas Rings (Munich), Holger Röder (Frankfurt), Michael Römer (Munich), Luca Rossi (Milan), Ilnort Rueda Saldivar (São Paulo), Ferdinand Salehi (Berlin), Oliver Scheel (Düsseldorf), Sieghart Scheiter (Düsseldorf), Bernd Schmidt (Düsseldorf), Jörg Schrottke (Munich), Christian Schuh (Vienna), Helmut Schulte-Croonenberg (Düsseldorf), Otto Schulz (Düsseldorf), Nikolaus Soellner (Düsseldorf), Martin Sonnenschein (Berlin), Jiri Steif (Prague), Torsten Stocker (Hong Kong), Markus Stricker (Zürich), Michael Strohmer (Vienna), Manfred Türks (Zürich), Patrick Van den Bossche (Washington, D.C.), Mirko Warschun (Munich), Mark van Weegen (Atlanta), Michael Weiss (Istanbul), Ingo Willems (Düsseldorf), Branko Zibret (Vienna).

We appreciate the countless people who every year helped to organize the Best Innovator competitions in their local markets while applying the Best Innovator knowledge. leaders include, among others: Par Aström (Stockholm), Edson Bauer (São Paulo), Peter van den Brande (Brussels), Sohin Chinoy (Washington, D.C.), Tomislav Čorak (Ljubljana), Jose Roberto Dalmolim (São Paulo), Sebastian Drescher (Munich), Elisabeth Easton (London), Soeren Grabowski (Moscow), Igor Hulak (Prague), Lenka Krobova (Prague), Fredrik Lannerberth (Copenhagen), Christian Loy (Düsseldorf), Luca Olivari (Rome), Charles Perrard (Paris), Ingo Petersen (Munich), Etienne Sebaux (Paris), Nicolas Sultan (Paris), Reine Wasner (Zürich), Espen Wiik (Oslo), and Matthias Witzemann (Vienna).

Finally, thanks to those who shared their expertise during the writing, editing, and publishing process: Eva Diedrichs, Martin Ruppert, and Patricia Sibo. We are grateful to Kevin McDermott for his help in writing the book and hours spent performing additional research, and to our former colleague and co-author Stephen Dyer for sharing ideas and examples from his many years in the innovation arena. We are indebted to Martin Liu and Laura Hawkins at LID for their enthusiastic support and close cooperation.

REFERENCES

1   Edward Lawler and Chris Worley, *Built to Change: How to Achieve Sustained Organizational Effectiveness*, Jossey-Bass, 2006

2   "Regional Highlights: Latin America," Whirlpool Corporation 2013 Annual Report

3   "Whirlpool Latin America Report 2011," Whirlpool's report to the United Nations Global Compact

4   "Tatas in contrarian mode, celebrate failures," *The Financial Express*, 3 May 2011

5   The phrase is usually attributed to Carlos Ghosn, president and CEO of Nissan. See *India Inside: The Emerging Innovation Challenge to the West* by Nirmalya Kumarand and Phanish Puranam (Harvard Business Press, p. 114).

6   The term "Black Swan" is taken from the book by Nassim Nicholas Taleb, *The Black Swan: The Impact of the Highly Improbable* (Random House, 2007). Taleb defines a Black Swan by three principal characteristics: it is unpredictable; it carries a massive impact; and, after the fact, we concoct an explanation that makes it appear less random, and more predictable, than it was.

7   Hofstede, Hofstede, and Minkov, *Cultures and Organizations: Software of the Mind* (third edition), McGraw-Hill, 2010

8   "An Innovation Leader," *Appliance Magazine*, April 2004

9   For an in-depth account of Shell's approach, see *The Art of the Long View: Planning for the Future in an Uncertain World* by Peter Schwartz (Doubleday, 1991). To see how Shell continues to apply its methodology, see "Shell Energy Scenarios to 2050" at www.shell.com.

10 See "Scenario-Based Strategic Planning in Times of Tumultuous Change" by Paul A. Laudicina, et al. (*A.T. Kearney Ideas & Insights*, February 2012).

11 Christensen, Clayton M., Cook, Scott, Hall, Taddy, "Marketing malpractice: the cause and the cure," Harvard Business Review, December 2005

12 Ulwick, Anthony W., *What Customers Want: Using Outcome-Driven Innovation to Create Breakthrough Products and Services*, McGraw Hill, 2005

13 Ades et al., "Implementing Open Innovation: The Case of Natura, IBM and Siemens," Journal of Technology Management & Innovation, Volume 8, Special Issue, 2013

14 K. Naughton, "The Race to Market the Connected Car," *Automotive News*, 10 January 2014

15 IMP³rove benchmarking database, 2013; N = 3,652

16 Reports from the Commission to the European Parliament, the Council, the European Economic Social Committee, and the Committee of the Regions; report of the European Commission, 30 January 2013

17 TGV is train à grande vitesse, or high-speed train.

18 L. Brown, "Business Models & Innovation: Interview with Barbara Dalibard, Managing Director, SNCF Voyages," *EURAILmag*, issue 22, 2014

19 Karim R. Lakhani and Jill A. Panetta, "The Principles of Distributed Innovation." *Innovations: Technology, Governance, Globalization*, volume 2, number 3, summer 2007

20 L. Brown, "Business Models & Innovation: Interview with Barbara Dalibard, Managing Director, SNCF Voyages," *EURAILmag*, issue 22, 2014; R. Bonazzi et al. "Respecting the Deal: Economically Sustainable Management of

Open Innovation Among Co-Opeting Companies," *International Journal of E-Services and Mobile Applications*, volume 4, issue 1, 2012

[21] For a general guide to sharing intellectual property in collaborations with external partners, see "Innovation in Multi-Invention Contexts: Mapping Solutions to Technological and Intellectual Property Complexity" by Deepak Somaya et al. in *California Management Review* (volume 53, number 4, summer 2011).

[22] "Innovative Products," www.henkel.com

[23] J. Howe, "The Rise of Crowdsourcing," *Wired Magazine*, June 2006

[24] Rushing et al., "Turbocharging Open Innovation in a 100-Day Blitz," *A.T. Kearney Ideas & Insights*, February 2013

[25] For an example from the hotel industry, see "Innovation: Are You Focused on the Perfect Over the Optimal?" by Sauvage et al. in A.T. Kearney Executive Agenda (January 2012).

[26] "Coca-Cola Set to Unleash Freestyle Drink Machine in 2010," *Vending Solutions*, 9 November 2009

[27] "Follow the Procurement Leaders: Assessment of Excellence in Procurement Study," *A.T. Kearney Ideas & Insights*, November 2011

[28] T.H. Davenport, "Saving IT's Soul: Human-Centered Information Management," Harvard Business Review, March 1994

[29] "Valeo highlighting its micro-hybrid solutions for the US market: i-StARS and ReStart," *Green Car Congress*, 28 February 2012

[30] Enrico & Kornbluth, *The Other Guy Blinked*, page 240, Bantam Books, 1986

[31] See *The Machine That Changed the World: The Story of Lean Production, Toyota's Secret Weapon in the Global Car Wars That Is Now Revolutionizing World Industry* by Womack, Jones, and Roos (Simon and Schuster, 1990).

[32] "MQB – der neue Modulare Querbaukasten," Volkswagen Internationaler Presseworkshop, February 2012

[33] L. Brown, "Business Models & Innovation: Interview with Barbara Dalibard, Managing Director, SNCF Voyages," *EURAILmag*, issue 22, 2014

[34] "3D Printing Scales Up," The Economist, 7 September 2013

[35] J.L. Seglin, "Hot Strategy: 'Be Unprofitable for a Long Time.'" Inc. Magazine, 1 September 1997

[36] P. Farhi, "Jeffrey Bezos, Washington Post's next owner, aims for a new 'golden era' at the newspaper," The Washington Post, 3 September 2013

[37] For more on matching leadership styles to the phases of an innovation strategy, see the typology proposed by Jean-Philippe Deschamps in "The Critical Attributes of Innovation Leaders" in the proceedings of the European Best Innovator Club annual meeting in 2008.

[38] See "Home-Grown CEO" by Fred Steingraber at www.atkearney.com (4 April 2011).

[39] Mahler, McDermott, and Walker, "Winning in a Turbulent World," A.T. Kearney Executive Agenda, November 2012

[40] Kaempfer, Peppard, and Violani, "Where Have All the 10-Year Strategies Gone?" A.T. Kearney, June 2011

KAI ENGEL is an A.T. Kearney partner and head of the firm's Innovation Practice for Europe. He has more than 20 years of consulting and industry expertise in all areas of innovation management, including innovation strategy, portfolio management, innovation-to-profit, and supplier-driven innovation.

In 2003, Kai initiated the firm's Best Innovator Competition and the Best Innovators Club, and for the past eight years has been a key collaborator with the EU Commission's IMP³rove initiative. He is the author of numerous articles and books, including German-language versions of *Innovation Management* and *Best Innovators—Successful Strategies of Innovation Leaders*. He also chairs executive roundtables and is a frequent presenter at business and industry conferences.

Kai earned a doctorate in mechanical engineering from the University of Hannover and a degree in business administration from the University of Braunschweig.

VIOLETKA DIRLEA is an A.T. Kearney partner and head of the firm's Innovation Practice for the Americas. She has more than 15 years of business and consulting experience, primarily in industrial manufacturing, with a focus on advising original equipment manufacturers and suppliers on how to improve performance.

Violetka's expertise extends to all areas of the value chain—from quality, innovation strategy, and supply chain strategy to profitability, organizational design, and cost and quality transformations—as she helps companies gain competitive advantage.

Violetka earned a dual master's degree in international business and business administration from Thunderbird, the American Graduate School of International Management, and Arizona State University.

JOCHEN GRAFF is an A.T. Kearney principal and member of the firm's Operations Practice, where he has a leadership role on the R&D and innovation management team. With more than 15 years of consulting experience, Jochen advises clients across industries on all topics related to innovation, R&D, and operations and shares his expertise in the engineering, automotive, high-tech, and process industries. Jochen coordinates the firm's annual Best Innovator Competition globally. He has published numerous articles on innovation management and is a frequent conference contributor.

Jochen earned graduate degrees in business administration from Erasmus University Rotterdam and the London School of Economics, where he earned the additional Community of European Management Schools (CEMS) degree.